CHICHESTER HARBOUR

A History

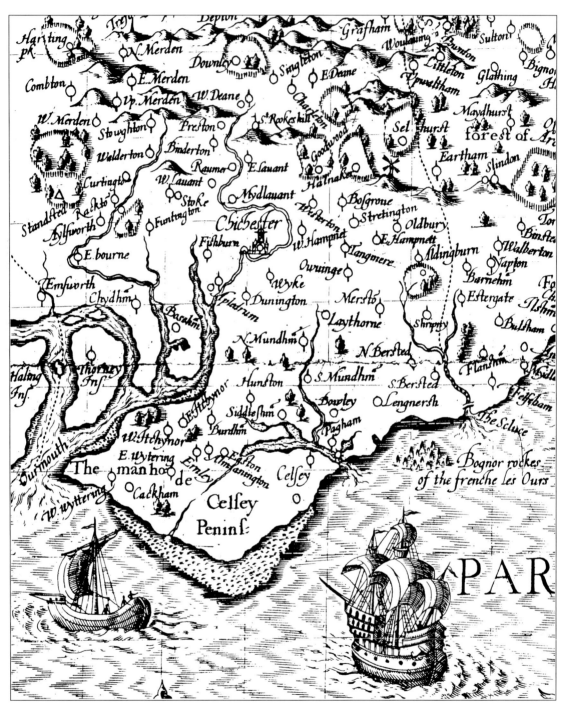

Detail from map of Sussex, 1595, by John Norden

CHICHESTER HARBOUR

A History

John Reger

Published to commemorate
the first twenty-five years
of the
Chichester Harbour Conservancy
1971 - 1996

Phillimore

1996

Published by
PHILLIMORE & CO. LTD.
Shopwyke Manor Barn, Chichester, West Sussex

ISBN 1 86077 019 3

Printed and bound in Great Britain by
BUTLER AND TANNER LTD.
London and Frome

Contents

*This history of Chichester Harbour is dedicated
to the memory of*

*Vice-Admiral Sir Geoffrey Thistleton-Smith, KBE, CB, GM, DL
First Chairman of the Chichester Harbour Conservancy
1971-1975*

List of Illustrations

Main front cover illustration: Bosham photographed by Iain McGowan, F.R.P.S.; insets: *Transit*, built at Itchenor, 1800; George Haines of Itchenor, harbour pilot, *c*.1940.

Back cover: Chichester Harbvour Federation has organised an annual regatta week, based on Hayling Island Sailing Club, since 1964. Of recent years over 300 dinghies and keelboats, racing in 14 classes, have taken part. The winners receive prize plates which depict the burgees of the 14 clubs in the harbour.

    The burgees on the back cover are arranged clockwise in the geographical order of the clubs around the harbour. Starting at 6 o'clock, being the harbour entrance, they represent: Chichester Cruiser Racing Club, Hayling Island Sailing Club, Mengham Rythe Sailing Club, Langstone Sailing Club, Emsworth Sailing Club, Emsworth Slipper Sailing Club, Emsworth Cruising Association, Thorney Island Sailing Club (Royal Air Force Sailing Association), Thorney Island Water Sports Centre (Royal Artillery Yacht Club), Bosham Sailing Club, Dell Quay Sailing Club, Chichester Yacht Club, Itchenor Sailing Club, West Wittering Sailing Club.

Foreword

by

His Grace the Duke of Richmond and Gordon

My family have been associated with Chichester Harbour for over two hundred years.

The 3rd Duke of Richmond bought land at West Itchenor in the late 18th century and built Itchenor House as his yachting lodge. He also installed a salt-water bath on the shore near where the Harbour Office now stands!

While Itchenor House was under construction, Goodwood House was extended, and the sloop *Goodwood* owned by the Duke brought tons of stone and bricks from Swanage, Guernsey and Plymouth for the building works, all shipped through Itchenor.

In more recent years my wife and I and our children have enjoyed the harbour from the land and water, and it has a special place in our memories and affections.

This new history of the harbour marks the 25th anniversary of the formation of the Chichester Harbour Conservancy, in whose safe hands the management of this internationally important area now lies.

I salute the Conservancy's achievements and its initiative in commissioning a book which I know will be much enjoyed by all those who, like me, know and love Chichester Harbour.

1   Toasting the Harbour. The Duke of Richmond watching Chichester Harbour Federation Regatta, 1994, with (right) Lieutenant-Colonel David Jones, Chairman of Chichester Harbour Conservancy.

Preface

Chichester Harbour must surely rank as one of the finest inland seascapes in the country. Set against the glorious backdrop of the South Downs and the lofty spire of Chichester Cathedral, its creeks and channels of tidal water make for an incomparable setting. As an Area of Outstanding Natural Beauty as well as a Site of Special Scientific Interest of international standing, the harbour is a mecca for all who love the sea and its shoreline countryside. There is so much for so many: for sailors, walkers, artists, bird-watchers, scientists and environmentalists and those in search of some quite remarkable history.

Chichester Harbour was once a waterway to history, its long fingers of water urging invaders and settlers deep into the landscape. The harbour led to one of the most important Roman sites in southern England and later to one of the earliest Christian sites in Sussex. And one of the essential prologues in the countdown to the Norman Conquest was played out on this harbourside. Then throughout subsequent centuries the harbour has played host to commerce and trade right up to the present century. Once it was wool, grain and coal, trade long since gone, but now there is the boat-building business of international repute that has grown up around the shores of the present-day harbour.

Today the Chichester Harbour Conservancy jealously guards its outstanding amenities as it has done for the past twenty-five years since its formation in 1971. It is to mark this silver jubilee in 1996 that this present history has been prepared.

It is a story of both land and water, about a complex inter-relationship that has varied throughout the centuries and that today is studied and respected by the Conservancy as a cornerstone of its management policy. The water cannot be divorced from the land.

This history attempts to weave together something of this delicate inter-relationship in both the past and the present. It is a history originally researched by John Reger of Emsworth. For many years he has studied and written about Havant and Emsworth and the Hampshire harbourside. What is presented here is the result of some thirty years work. As an original member of the Chichester Harbour Conservancy since 1971—representing Hampshire County Council—he has been actively involved in all aspects of its work and is close to many of the problems facing the harbour today.

John Reger's original draft was passed to Kim Leslie of the West Sussex Record Office who has been responsible for editing, redrafting and expanding the text and for gathering together a considerable collection of illustrative material from which a selection has been made for publication here, and for compiling the index.

The search for more material about the history of the harbour will continue after the publication of this book to help secure information and material that might otherwise be ultimately lost. Reminiscences, snaps from the family photographic album, random scraps of news, nothing is too trivial from which to piece together the human face of Chichester Harbour in the past. Offers of any information or assistance should be sent to the West Sussex Record Office where any new records gathered in will be preserved alongside those of the Chichester Harbour Conservancy which are also held here.

John Reger   Kim Leslie
Emsworth   West Sussex Record Office, Chichester

Acknowledgements

Many kind people around the harbour and beyond have made their own special contribution to this book. It has been very much a collaborative effort in many ways.

Thanks firstly must go to his Grace the Duke of Richmond for contributing his Foreword and to two leading members of Chichester Harbour Conservancy, Lieutenant-Colonel David Jones, its Chairman, and Sir Jeremy Thomas, Chairman of the Advisory Committee. Their enthusiastic support throughout this project has been backed by considerable help about the minutiae of Conservancy matters from John Godfrey, Deputy Clerk, and Paul Amis, Senior Administrative Officer. From the Harbour Office at Itchenor, Philip Couchman, the Environment Manager, has been ever-ready to share his deep knowledge of the harbour, as has Anne de Potier, the Conservancy's Conservation Warden.

So many have given generous help from the sharing of information and reminiscences to the loan of precious family photographs. In particular Bosham's local historian, Angela Bromley-Martin, has taken enormous trouble to answer queries, suggest contacts and make available her vast collection of harbour photographs. Geoffrey Godber, the Conservancy's first Clerk, who made such an important contribution to its creation, has thrown some interesting sidelights on the harbour's history and some of its personalities from his own unique perspective. Freddie Hard, the Conservancy's first Harbour Master, and Ann Fox, his secretary, have also helped with the early history of the new harbour authority in the '70s. Nigel Pusinelli has supplied information about Harbour Federation matters. Help has also been given by John Bartlett, David, Glenn and Robert Bowker, Captain David Bromley-Martin, Patricia Combes, Simon Combes, Tessa Daines, Lieutenant-Commander Neil Edden, Rear-Admiral Philip Gick, George and Kenneth Haines, Rex and Julia Hawkins, Sheila and Roy Morgan, Jerome O'Hea, Frank Parham, Strahan Soames and Tony Yoward.

Several of the harbour's sailing clubs were approached to add a flavour of their activities and information was gratefully received from the clubs at Bosham, Dell Quay, the two Emsworth clubs, Hayling Island, Itchenor and Mengham Rythe. Birdham Shipyard and the Hayling Yacht Company were also most helpful, as were the museums in Chichester, Emsworth and Havant. All three museums kindly permitted the copying of material in their care, as did the following who loaned photographs for copying: Angela Bromley-Martin, Geoffrey Godber, George Haines, Freddie Hard, Boo Mackay, John Morley, Michael Peacock, Alan Phillips, Nigel Pusinelli, Archie Shaw and Dave Turner.

A great deal of information has been quarried from Portsmouth Central Library, Portsmouth City Records Office, the Public Record Office, and also from the West Sussex Record Office, the Hampshire Record Office and Worthing Library. Photographs and documents from these last three have been reproduced with the kind permission of the respective County Archivists, Richard Childs and Rosemary Dunhill, and the West Sussex County Librarian, Robert Kirk. Martin Hayes, Local Studies Librarian in West Sussex, gave much help in the selection of harbour photographs kept in Worthing Library.

Permission to use copyright material has been given by Portsmouth Publishing and Printing Ltd of the News Centre, and for the use of Arthur Ransome material permission has been given by John Bell, Ransome's literary executor, and Leeds University Library where Ann Farr has been most helpful.

Drawings of two archaeological reconstructions have been contributed by Jill Dickin and Richard Lally, and Richard has also drawn four specially commissioned maps for the book. Also within the text have been inserted some excerpts about the Vietnamese refugees at Thorney by Daphne Byrne, the Men of Bosham by Kim Leslie and Arthur Ransome in the harbour by Roger Wardale.

On the production side many thanks are owed to photographer David Nicholls who has so skilfully copied all the early photographs and documents used as well as taking the many photographs of buildings and views around the harbour in the autumn of 1995. The original drafts for the book were expertly typed by Suzanne Elliott of the West Sussex County Council's Word Processing Centre at County Hall. Grateful thanks are also extended to Jenni Leslie for correcting the proofs and to the publishers, especially Noel Osborne, the Managing Director, and Nicola Willmot, Production Manager, for all their help and advice.

I

The Creation of the Harbour

What determines why men choose to settle in any given place is the geography and the geology that exists there. What early man needed, once he had become a farmer and not simply a hunter, was a combination of good soil, free, pure, and preferably spring water, and the possibility of easy communications so that trade between his community and his neighbours could develop. Additional incentives, especially in the early stages, were abundance of game, timber for houses and a plentiful supply of fish in the local seas and streams. All these factors existed in the region of Chichester Harbour.

The harbour itself came into being as a result of the changes in world temperature which began some 20,000 years ago as the last Ice Age ended. At that time Britain was still a part of the European land mass. In those days, down the centre of what is now the English Channel, flowed a river which archaeological geographers have called the Greater Seine, making its way

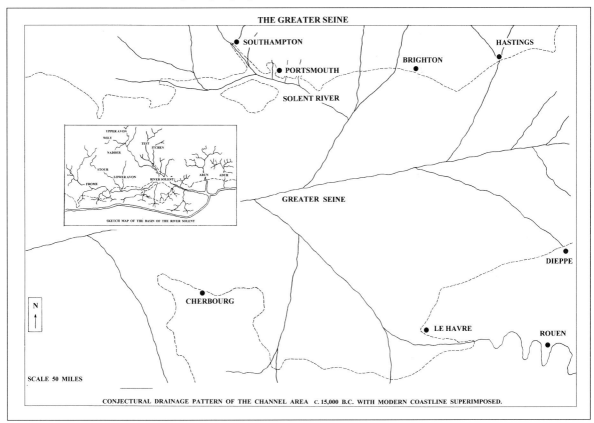

CONJECTURAL DRAINAGE PATTERN OF THE CHANNEL AREA c.15,000 B.C. WITH MODERN COASTLINE SUPERIMPOSED.

westward to join an Atlantic Ocean some 300 feet below its modern level. Into the Greater Seine flowed the rivers of northern France and southern England. One of these, today usually called the Solent river, followed the channels now occupied by the Solent and Spithead, joining the Greater Seine somewhere south of the present position of Arundel. The headwaters of the Solent river included the Dorset Stour and Avon, the Test and Itchen, the Hamble, the Meon and the three rivers flowing north from the Isle of Wight. Finally, there were three streams which originated in part from the springs which rise around Portsdown, in part from the lavant streams which flow from the south slope of the Downs. The three harbours of Portsmouth, Langstone and Chichester are the drowned upper reaches of these three river systems. The original appearance of the land formations through which the three ran must have been very close to what we can see today at low tide, with the spinal channels being the rivers, and the drying mudflats and saltings being the low-lying flat plains of gravel and brickearth covered with sparse vegetation.

As the earth grew warmer the ice-caps melted and sea levels rose. First, what we now know as Great Britain became an island, then, perhaps some 5,000-6,000 years ago, the chalk ridge between the Needles and Old Harry Rocks was breached. By the Bronze Age, Spithead and the Solent had effectively replaced the prehistoric Solent river, although these channels were still much narrower than they are today, with the northern shore lying perhaps a mile to the south of the modern coastline. With the relative rise in sea level caused by the melting of the polar ice, the rate of flow of the streams decreased and they became both wider and shallower. In this way the harbours began to take on their modern appearance. This process was to take

3   *The creeks and harbours of Chichester Harbour are the drowned upper reaches of ancient river systems.*

centuries—indeed to some extent it still continues—but perhaps by the end of the Middle Ages the general outline of the harbour as we see it today had emerged.

That the formation of the harbour took so long is due to the fact that the change in relative sea level was not one of continuous rise; there were numerous fluctuations and at times, what is dry land today, would have disappeared beneath the waters for centuries at a time. The particular picture that emerges for our area is one in which, some 4,000 years ago, sea level was some six feet lower than it is today. During the next 1,000 years there was a considerable rise, and much of the harbour area would have been submerged, with a number of islands and sandbanks in their place. By Roman times the waters had receded once more and were now back to where they had been some 2,000 years earlier. As sea level fell the ebb scoured the channels more thoroughly, and it was possible for vessels to penetrate as far inland as the Roman Landing at Fishbourne. It is difficult to say where exactly the coastline lay in Roman times, but it is likely to have comprised a series of low-lying islands and sandbanks one or two miles to the south of the present shore, with more permanent lands and islands within the harbours. From the time of the Roman invasion, until just before the Norman Conquest, sea levels rose; the outer islands and sandbanks were overwhelmed and a more stable shoreline was formed. This relative rise of the sea was slow at first, but from the fifth century seems to have increased. As the islands off the Dutch/Friesian coast were increasingly invaded by the North Sea, their original inhabitants, our Anglo-Saxon ancestors, were encouraged to seek other lands elsewhere. By the early 11th century the whole coast of southern Britain was subjected to increasing inundation, culminating in the Great Flood of 1048 when Selsey Island was over-flowed and the Saxon cathedral abandoned.

We must always be careful to distinguish between 'erosion', that is, the actual loss of land, and 'inundation', where lands were flooded but could subsequently be reclaimed; medieval documents are imprecise as to what they mean by 'losses to the sea'.

For almost 250 years, from the Great Flood of 1048, there seems to have been a virtual stand-still in sea level; indeed there may even have been a fall. Because of this, and because larger ships were now being built, it became increasingly difficult to bring trading vessels up to the heads of the harbours. Hence the development of Portsmouth in the late 12th century, the founding of Emsworth in 1239, and the emergence of Dell Quay as the port for Chichester in the early 13th century.

By the late 13th century the sea was once more rising, and rising rapidly. From the time when Old Winchelsea was drowned in 1297, until well into the 15th century, there are numerous claims from the harbourside communities that land had been 'lost to the sea'. Much of this loss appears to have been within the harbour, for the rising waters caused the ebb to 'back up' and overflow the lower lying islands and shorelines; for example, there were some 40 acres lost in Thorney Island in the period between 1300 and 1340. There is also evidence of land loss along the coast as well, though how far to the south the 14th-century coastline lay it is impossible to say; estimates have ranged from under a mile to four or five, but the lower figure would appear to be more likely.

The harbour that the first settlers found lay on the southern edge of the Hampshire Basin; along the shore the soil is a light and easily worked brickearth, described by one authority as 'one of the finest light soils in Britain'. It was particularly suitable for primitive agriculture. In early times a belt of woodland was growing on the heavy clay soils which separate the Downs from the coastal plain. Through this woodland there were only a few natural routes: one passed north from Havant through Rowlands Castle along the line now followed by the railway, and another followed the Lavant valley, north of Chichester. For the dwellers on the coastlands the forests provided both protection from the north, timber for various purposes, and wasteland where they could pasture their cattle and swine. The real advantage of the coastlands, however, is the abundance of springs which lie in a continuous line from Bedhampton eastwards.

The water which rises from them comes from the rain which falls on the Downs and sinks into the chalk strata which dips beneath the clay, the northern edge of which runs from Horndean, through Hambrook, to just north of Chichester. The most northerly belt is that of

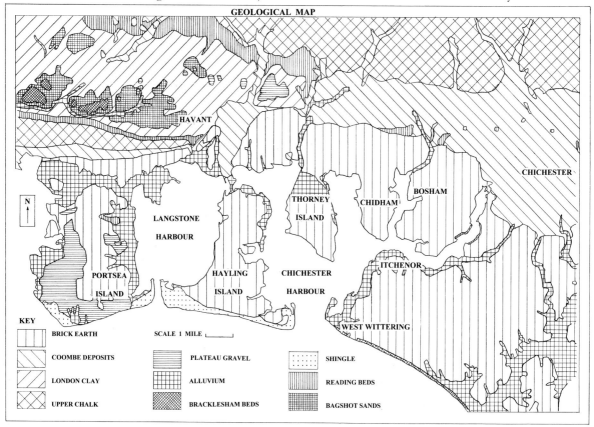

the Reading Beds, then come the London Clay outcrop, a narrow band of Bagshot Sands and, finally, the sands and gravels of the Bracklesham Beds. Pushing up through these clays, and of great importance to the local geological structure, is the chalk of the Portsdown Inlier which stretches for some 20 miles from Knowle, near Fareham, to Apuldram and Stockbridge, near Chichester. This geological feature is like an iceberg, in that only the ridge of Portsdown is visible, yet from the crest of that hill the chalk masked by layers of gravel and brickearth stretches south for some two miles into Portsea Island, whilst the eastward continuation, ranging in width from two miles to less than one, runs under the superficial deposits well into the Man-hood peninsula. To the north of Portsdown the outcrops of Bracklesham Clay are, on the whole, above the water-table in the chalk, but to the east the southern edge of the clay is below that water-table; this is the reason for the line of springs which stretches from the base of Portsdown well into Sussex. Without the inlier there would have been a far poorer water supply and the history of the harbour area would have been very different. In the past the water from these springs and from the lavants has been the only source of land drainage replenishment for all three harbours; today much of this spring water is abstracted by the water company, which may eventually have an adverse effect on the harbour's ability to continue in being.

Brickearth lying on top of chalk appears to be the most fertile of the various local soils. As an example of this, in 1939, land in North Hayling produced the highest yield of wheat per arable acre in all England.

The soil least favoured by our agricultural ancestors was brickearth on top of Reading Clay. The outcrop of this stratum, hidden by its cover of drift deposits, is about a mile wide. In

5   The ancient harbourside forest looking across Fishbourne Channel from Salterns Copse to Old Park Wood.

Chichester Harbour the northern edge runs from Tye in Hayling Island to a point just south of Dell Quay and on into the Manhood. This strip remained tree-covered long after lands to the north and south had been cleared; the woodland marked the division of Hayling into the two communities of North i'the Wood, and South i'the Wood, but whilst there are occasional trees still standing along its course, the only surviving remnant of the forest which covered the Reading Clay is Old Park Wood in the east of the Bosham peninsula. The Romans made much use of this red clay for pottery, tiles and bricks, and traces of a tilery have been recently uncovered in the Reading Beds area just south of Dell Quay.

The London Clay subsoil occupies most of the rest of the land around the harbour, apart from a strip some half a mile wide bordering the actual coast where the underlying strata are formed by the sands and gravels of the Bracklesham Beds. Today most of this strip is uncultivated, forming the Beachlands and Common in Hayling Island and the car park at West Wittering.

The streams which rise on the Downs themselves, and flow over the clay towards the harbour, tend today to be lavants or winterbournes, and only flow when the water-table in the chalk reaches a sufficient level. Although it is not unlikely that in the past they flowed constantly, nowadays they can be dry for years at a stretch; then comes a period of unusually heavy rainfall, the lavants rise and serious flooding occurs, as it did in early 1994 when the Chichester Lavant rose in its bed, flooded the villages in its downland valley and threatened to swamp part of the city itself. Other lavants feed the upper reaches of the Ems; in 1994 the road through the village of Stoughton became a watercourse, and Walderton and Westbourne, too, were badly affected. The third lavant flows through Havant to enter Langstone Harbour. By 1994 there had been some 20 years without a drop of water passing Idsworth Chapel, but in that year the road from Chalton to Finchdean was six inches deep in places, and worse in others. The fourth major watercourse which rises in the chalk directly is the Bosham Millstream; its headwaters are the springs in the parish of Funtington, and there is nearly always some water north of West Ashling, save in the driest of years.

On the whole the flow of fresh water from the land into Chichester Harbour in any normal year is small if we compare the amount with the volume contained at high tide by the 11 square miles of water. What keeps the entrance clear is the force of the ebb tide as the harbour empties. The bed at the entrance is sandy with a degree of mud and clay; what sweeps out to sea is far from being the crystal spring water which enters it, hence the Saxon name for the harbour entrance, 'the Hormouth'—or 'Dirty Mouth'—to describe its coloration. One of the problems which faces the Conservancy is the need to keep this entrance clear and the bar sufficiently low for the vessels which regularly use the harbour to enter at most states of the tide. In this respect Portsmouth, with a gravel bed at its entrance, is more fortunate than either Langstone or Chichester. One reason for the latter's decline as a commercial port in the 19th century was the fact that the larger vessels then coming into use could no longer cross the bar except at high tide.

As sea levels rise, as we are told they are doing, various changes will ultimately occur. One may be that there will be flooding within the harbour. A second effect could be that the scouring of the entrance will decrease, which means that the bar will grow, gradually closing off the harbour mouth. The waters will become shallower, the scouring of the entrance will further decline and what was once a navigable haven could become a shallow lagoon and then dry land.

It is not just nature that has formed today's harbours; man, too, has taken a hand, although not always successfully. In the years after the battle of Waterloo there was an attempt to reclaim almost 300 acres of land at the northern end of Bosham Channel, but in the summer of 1822 a storm swept away a considerable portion of the embankment. It had been over 500 yards long and 15 feet high. The remains can still be seen today. There have been successes too: in 1870 the Deeps, which separated Thorney Island from Prinsted, were reclaimed, whilst more recently, lands once 'lost to the sea' on the eastern shore of Hayling have been similarly restored to agriculture.

To return to the question as to why men first came to live on the shores of Chichester Harbour, and why a port developed there. Firstly, the local soils were fertile and easy to work; secondly, there was an abundance of good spring water; thirdly, the harbour was rich in wildfowl, fish and shellfish; fourthly, the woodland provided building material for homes and pasture for pigs and cattle; lastly, there was a degree of access to the Downs, whence would come wool and wool-fells to be processed in both Chichester and Havant. As time progressed, the fertile soil provided a surplus of grain for the London market, in addition to the wool, cloth and leather already produced. Though no major river flowed into the harbour, denying full access to the interior, the Port of Chichester could flourish until the coming of the railways and the build up of the bar caused trade to decline. Until then, the port was successful and the reason for this was the nature of the harbour and the geological and geographical features which had formed it.

II

Permanent Settlements –
Prehistoric, Roman and Saxon

Early man was primarily a wanderer and left few reminders of his passing; however, as the pattern of his movements tended to be repeated down the years he left one permanent piece of evidence, the trackways which he followed in his annual nomadic round. By the end of the Mesolithic period, in about 2,500 BC, it is likely that the ridgeways along both Portsdown and the South Downs themselves were already ancient. There was also the track which skirted the heads of the creeks from Arundel to the three harbours and the various pathways through the forest which linked the coastland to the Downs. One passed over the Wadeway from Hayling Island through Havant to the chalk slopes above Rowlands Castle. Another would have gone from the shore at Fishbourne north along the Lavant valley to the Trundle and the flint mines just to the south-west. Along these trackways would have passed the trade goods of the time, salt, stone axeheads, flint tools and skins. The port of Chichester was already in being.

Bronze-Age man lived chiefly on the Downs, but by the early Iron Age, about 500 BC, agricultural techniques had improved sufficiently to enable men to start to clear the coastlands. In the vicinity of Chichester Harbour the principal early Iron-Age site is the Trundle. This had been constructed in the first place by Neolithic men as a causewayed camp, but from the fifth century BC onwards it was reoccupied and may well have developed into the equivalent of a 'town', a centre of trade and manufacture. By the middle of the first century BC it was obviously still of considerable importance. The Belgic tribe which had invaded the coastal plain from the west in the years after Caesar's first invasion built a series of earthworks north of the site of Chichester as if to protect some local base. This was either at Fishbourne or Chichester, or—as some have suggested because of the numbers of artefacts washed out of the shoreline of Bracklesham—perhaps at Selsey, though no actual site has ever been discovered there. This tribe was a branch of the Belgic Atrebates who had moved eastward when the greater part of their fellows had moved north up the Itchen valley to Winchester and the Hampshire uplands.

Other Iron-Age remains are to be found in Hayling Island. One of these is the 'fort' at Tourner Bury in the south-eastern corner of the island. From that site it would have been possible perhaps to have seen the mouth of the harbour and to have provided a place from which to warn of attacks from the sea. Excavations carried out in 1959 and 1971 found pre-Roman shards under the rampart and some Roman pottery fragments within the enclosure. It has been suggested that the work dates from about 200 BC and that even in Roman times it was occupied, perhaps as an outpost of Portchester Castle.

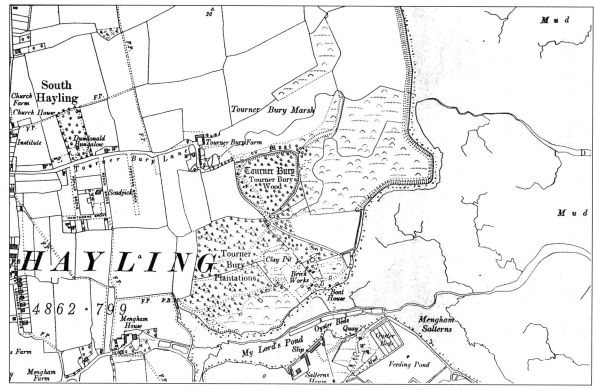

6 *Iron-Age harbourside look-out, Hayling Island. At Tourner Bury are the remains of a fortified encampment.*
(From Ordnance Survey 6" map, surveyed 1907.)

7 *Touncil Field Romano-British temple, Hayling Island. This conjectural drawing by Jill Dickin shows a circular temple within a colonnade.*

The second of Hayling's Iron-Age sites lies in the north, in what was once called 'the Touncil Field'. Here, local legend had it, a 'Great House' had once stood. Towards the end of the last century Dr. Talfourd Ely conducted a series of excavations and came to the conclusion that most of the work was Roman, but could not decide to what use the building had been put. Following the drought of 1976, which revealed the building's foundations in the form of crop marks, a second series of excavations was carried out. The results were to prove that the building had been built in two stages: in the late Iron Age it had been a votive shrine where sacrifices of pigs and horses and gifts of coins had been made. In Roman times a circular temple with a colonnade had replaced the earlier structure and remained in use during that period of history.

The Belgae and the Romans are known to have traded with one another, so we may presume that commerce existed between the harbour and northern France in the years immediately prior to the Claudian invasion. From archaeological evidence it looks as if the inward trade was in precious metals and similar luxuries. Exports no doubt consisted of hides and leather, perhaps some corn and most probably salt, for there is evidence all round the harbour in the form of briquetage, those patches of reddish burnt earth seen along the shoreline, showing that prehistoric man made concentrations of brine during the summer and then boiled it in heavy earthenware pots in the autumn. Camden in his *Britannia* quotes St Augustine as saying that the salt produced in this region was superior to that produced anywhere else in Britain, so we must assume that the industry also continued after the Conquest of AD 49.

At the time of this invasion the area around Chichester was ruled by a chieftain called Cogidubnus. The Romans called him a king, his territory a kingdom—or Regnum—and his

8 *Roman wall, Chichester. The Bishop's Palace bastion near the south-west corner of the city.*

people the Regni. Cogidubnus is said to have been Rome's ally; certainly the Romans treated him well and his capital was rebuilt in the Roman fashion and given the name *Noviomagus Regnensium*—the new market of the people of the kingdom.

Evidence suggests that the Romans had a landing place or mini-port at the head of the Fishbourne Channel and built a military base there; it was probably a supply depot initially, designed to give logistic support to the Roman campaign in the West Country. There may even have been some kind of fort at Chichester, but the latter soon developed into a civil township, whilst sometime after the death of Cogidubnus the famous Flavian palace was built on the Fishbourne site.

The Roman occupation produced a dual culture with a civilised Romano-British population living in the towns and country villas, and a native British culture living in the more remote areas. Around the harbour it was the Roman element which prevailed. Clustered along the line

9   *Roman Harbour Meadows, Fishbourne. These meadows at the head of Fishbourne Channel are reputedly the site, long since silted up, of the harbour that supplied the nearby Roman palace.*

10   *Fishbourne Roman sea-horse. The finest Roman mosaic in the palace was inspired by the sea. A winged cupid riding a dolphin is surrounded by four sea-beasts: two winged sea-horses and two winged sea-panthers. Strategically positioned at the head of the harbour, the maritime influence on Roman life here must have been considerable.*

of the roads they built are a number of so-called 'villa' sites. The chief of these roads from the point of view of the harbour was that which ran from Chichester to Havant; on the Sussex side the alignment has not been fully traced, but from Emsworth to Havant it followed more or less the present A259. At Havant, almost certainly the site of a posting station or small town, the road changed its alignment to pass north of Portsdown Hill on its way to Bitterne or Winchester. This alteration can still be seen today by anyone who stands outside the *Bear Hotel* in East Street, Havant.

From Chichester further metalled roads radiated, the most important from the Roman point of view being Stane Street to London, but there were others, one in the direction of Silchester, a second eastwards to Arundel and a third south into the Manhood. The metalled roads were not the only lines of communication; gravelled tracks also existed and seem to have

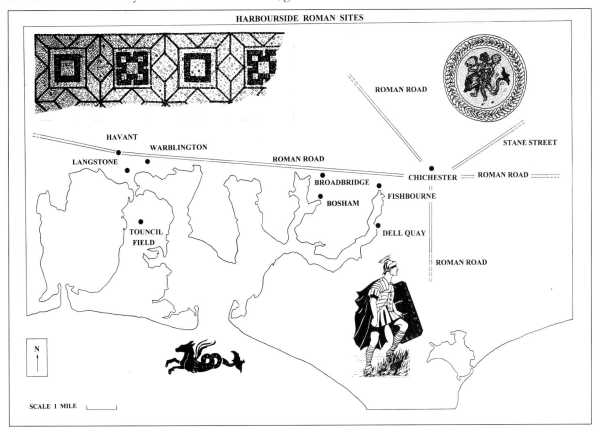

11

been well used. One went north from Hayling Island over the Wadeway through Havant to Rowlands Castle; another seems to have passed south through Broadbridge to Bosham; there may even have been a link to Birdham. Such an elaborate network was presumably to enable a proportion of the surplus corn grown on the coastal plain to be exported to Gaul and the Rhine garrisons.

If Chichester was the chief market town in Roman days, then Havant was already of some importance with its road junction, its connection with the temple at Hayling Island, and its port at Langstone. There are a number of Roman sites in that immediate area. In the 1920s a building with a hypocaust—the Roman form of central heating—was found south of the town;

more recently there have been further finds along the line of the old Hayling railway. It has also been suggested that St Faith's church stands on a Roman foundation. There have been other recent discoveries at Langstone and in the burial ground at Warblington, whilst there is a further site, to date unexcavated, in the fields of Warblington Castle Farm where surface finds after ploughing would indicate the presence of floors paved with tesserae and probably a heating system.

12   *The Romans at Bosham. Many Roman finds have been uncovered near the church such as this colossal marble head from a Roman statue.*

On the Sussex side of the harbour, too, there are similar structures, from the 'villas' at Broadbridge and Sidlesham to the tile works at Dell Quay and the evidence of a Roman presence at Bosham. The first two centuries of Roman Britain appear to have been a time of increasing prosperity and general security. Chichester remained unwalled, its population approaching 2,000. To its markets came not just foreign merchants but Celtic farmers from the downland area anxious to exchange their surplus products for the comforts of civilisation. Imports through the harbour would have continued to have been largely in luxuries: wine, samian ware and possibly even silks and dyed cloths. Exports would have been grain, wool, hides and salt. Perhaps there was even a foreign market for the coarse local earthenware made at, amongst other places, Rowlands Castle where the Reading Clay was fired in a reducing furnace to produce a fine greyish ware found at most of the local Roman sites.

Towards the end of the second century Roman Britain suffered a shock; the Picts broke through the northern defences, and even towns in the south, such as Chichester, built walls for their own protection. By the middle of the third century attacks on the civilised world were increasing; by about AD 300 the walls of Chichester had been strengthened in thickness and bastions had been added. To this period, too, dates the construction of the Saxon Shore forts such as that at Portchester.

From the third century onwards life in Roman Britain became more precarious; the villas and buildings nearest to the coast became increasingly vulnerable and were abandoned; life in the provinces tended to become concentrated in the towns, and this appears to be particularly true of Chichester and the Sussex coastal plain, where rural buildings seem either to have been burnt, or allowed to fall into decay, whilst in Chichester the early fourth century seems to have been one of increased civic activity. Perhaps one might suggest that the fate of the great Fishbourne Palace to some extent mirrors the changes of these times. In the late second century the building was entirely remodelled and brought up to date with new floors and heating systems. By the early years of the third century a comfortable modernised house stood on the site; some fifty to sixty years later the whole of the north wing was destroyed by fire. The site seems to have been abandoned, to be used as a quarry, although squatters may have camped in the ruins of the east wing. By the time of the Saxon invasion the 'palace' would have virtually disappeared.

The Roman legions finally left Britain in the early years of the fifth century. The new invaders, the Angles, Saxons and Jutes, seem to have completed their colonisation by the early years of the sixth century. During this 'Dark Age' it would appear that the pattern of trade and industry and the whole aspect of town life disappeared. In Chichester there is a degree of archaeological evidence to suggest that urban decay had set in by the mid-fifth century and that the town was virtually derelict by the time the legendary Cissa took it over some time after AD 500. It is now generally agreed that the occupation of Wessex was carried out by Saxons who had seized the Thames valley and had moved west and south from Berkshire. Those who occupied the Isle of Wight and then moved into southern Hampshire are thought to have been Jutes; other members of the same tribe, the Meonwara, moved inland along the Meon valley and apparently did not come very much further to the east. The people who took Sussex did so from the sea. It used to be thought that their traditional landing place of 'Cymenes-ora' was either at Selsey or in the area of Chichester Harbour, but one modern researcher has suggested that it was further to the east, and that the South Saxons first consolidated their hold on the area around Pevensey in about 490, and then moved west towards Chichester and Havant. This idea would mean that there could have been a Romano-British enclave surviving until the end of the century, a suggestion which is perhaps supported by the evidence of the place-name of Havant, which was anciently 'Hama's Funta', the place of Hama's spring—where 'Funta' is a Romano-British survival—and the various prefixes of 'Wealh', seen in places such as Walton Farm in Bosham, Walesworth, a lost village on the north slope of Portsdown Hill, and Wellsworth, to the north of Rowlands Castle.

13 The Saxons in Chichester Harbour. Warblington church was originally built by the Saxon invaders that penetrated the harbour. The centre stage of the tower with its little Saxon window is all that survives from this period.

Christianity seems to have come late to Sussex, for although Bede speaks of the hermit Dicul already in his cell at Bosham when Wilfred came in 681, it was not until after this date that the South Saxons renounced their pagan gods and the cathedral was established at Selsey to be the mother church of the district.

If we study the evidence of the place-names and the surviving Saxon charters it is possible to give a rough estimate of when the Saxons made their various settlements around the harbour. Modern research tends to think that the earliest settlements would have been made on lands once tilled during the Roman period, and that they tend to end in '-ham'. Thus we would suspect that Bosham would have been amongst the earliest Saxon villages on the shores of the harbour. The second group of settlements tends to have the suffix '-ing' or '-ington'. Thus Hayling Island, 'the island of Haegel's people', Warblington, the 'town of Weorbel's people', and the Witterings would also be among the earlier places taken over by the invaders. The

Saxon charter which gave the Island of Selsey to Wilfred confirms that Birdham and Itchenor were already in existence by that date as both places are mentioned by name. By inference from Domesday Book we can conclude that most of the other places around the harbour had been occupied by 1086, even though their names do not emerge until the 12th or 13th centuries. The sole exception is Emsworth; there is no mention of the place in the Conqueror's great survey and no other reference which can be identified as being Emsworth. The name first appears in the 12th century, but its real existence as a place of some importance dates from 1239 when the lord of the manor obtained a charter for a fair and a market.

By the mid-ninth century Saxon England seems to have settled down to a degree of order, with the Wessex kings becoming increasingly important. The population was now perhaps half what it had been at the time of the Roman occupation and the old patterns of trade and industry had declined; gradually a degree of economic life was returning and Chichester seems once more to have been an urban centre. Then came that series of Danish invasions which threatened once more to destroy the hegemony of Wessex. King Alfred eventually came to power and to defend his people he both 'shired' the Kingdom and created the fortified centres or burghs on which he based his defences. In West Sussex one obvious choice was Chichester with its circuit of Roman walls, recently repaired by the Saxons. An attack by the Danes on the harbour communities was driven off successfully by 'the townsmen of Chichester' in 895—presumably by all the able-bodied men in the neighbourhood. There followed almost a century of peace until Ethelred II became king in 978. In 1000 the Anglo-Saxon Chronicle records that 'everywhere in Sussex, and in Hampshire and also in Berkshire they plundered and burned as their custom is....', and we may be sure that the townships around the harbour suffered similarly. In Bosham they still tell the story of how, when the Danes raided, they stole a bell from the church, only to lose it during their flight when its weight upset their boat off 'the bell hole'. An interesting story, but probably apocryphal; Saxon bells were mostly small and not cast but made of folded metal. They were hand bells, and light. Not until the mid-11th century are cast bells found, and not until much later were they of any size. The belfry of Bosham church is thought to have been completed at about the end of the 10th century so it is just possible that a bell could have been hung there and stolen, but unlikely to have been large enough to upset a Danish longship.

When Canute came to the throne in 1016 and restored order to the land, Bosham became an important place. Originally a manor belonging to the Archbishop of Canterbury, it was acquired, perhaps by a somewhat devious ploy, by Godwin, Canute's chief supporter in Sussex whom he made Earl of Wessex. After Canute's death Bosham became a principal, even the favourite, seat of the Godwin family, and the great Earl seems to have been responsible for determining the succession of the next three rulers of England. During the Confessor's reign, first Earl Godwin himself and, after his death his son, Harold, were the real rulers of the country, resented by the other great noblemen and feared by the king, whose wife was Godwin's daughter. The Confessor liked neither the lady nor the married state; his interests lay with religion, his tastes with the family of his Norman mother. Whenever he could he did his best to strip the Godwins of power but he always failed. In 1049, during one of these problems, Swein Godwinson, the eldest son, was banished. In times of trouble the Godwins went to Bosham, and Swein turned up there with eight ships. He then went to Pevensey to ask his cousin Bjorn to try to persuade Edward to repeal the banishment; Bjorn came back to Bosham with Swein, to be murdered by Swein's men. Swein was declared an outlaw, fled to Flanders, went on a crusade and died, and Harold became his father's heir.

14   Prelude to 1066. Scene from the Bayeux Tapestry showing Harold praying at Bosham church before he set sail for Normandy in 1064.

In 1052 Godwin fell from power and went abroad; his family concentrated at its Bosham base. Next year Godwin was back in control, but died shortly afterwards and Harold succeeded. It is as well to examine just how much of the harbour area the family controlled in the years before 1066. Bosham manor was immense, stretching as far north as Funtington and West Stoke; it also included Old Fishbourne, Chidham and land in the Manhood as far south as Birdham and Itchenor. Elsewhere the Godwins held Westbourne, Warblington, Singleton and New Fishbourne. The Witterings, most of Hayling Island and the lands of Bosham church were under ecclesiastic control, and Harold controlled the bishops. He had even 'seized' Eastoke in Hayling Island on the eve of the invasion to make certain that he could control the entrance to the harbour. The lands around Bosham were the key to his kingdom.

It was from Bosham that Harold sailed to Normandy in 1064. Having been tricked into taking an oath he was pledged to support William's claim to the English throne. The event, and Bosham church, are clearly shown on the Bayeux Tapestry. Following the battles of the autumn of 1066 and Harold's death, William redistributed the lands around the harbour. How they developed thereafter is another story.

III

Urban Occupations – Chichester and Havant

Alan Everitt, writing in the periodical *The Local Historian* in 1975, divided the market towns of England into three categories: firstly came medieval 'new or planted towns', that is, towns especially created to provide a market centre; into the second category came some villages—'upgraded villages'—which slowly developed into market towns by reason of their position in the land, or by the luck that their lord was powerful enough to obtain a market charter for them; thirdly came what he called 'primary towns', settlements of ancient foundation often associated with Roman roads or settlements. Into this category must fall Chichester with its Roman walls and tradition of urban occupation, and the much smaller settlement at Havant, built on a prehistoric cross-road site and probably permanently settled from Roman times onwards.

It has been said that in the Middle Ages all towns are villages, but not all villages are towns; the distinction between the two is not one of size but of function. The town is firstly the place where the produce of the countryside is processed and then sold on, either back to the villagers who produced it in the first place, or to other towns or even countries; secondly, the town is a place of trade with fairs and markets; thirdly, the town is a seat of administration both of the Church and the State.

At the time of the post-Conquest settlement, Chichester fulfilled all three of these functions: it was the largest town in Sussex, the head of a rape, the seat of a bishop and adjacent to a harbour of considerable size. By the 12th century it had a market granted for both Wednesday and Saturday, and the bishop had established his Sloe Fair by 1107-8. It was no doubt its importance as an administrative centre, rather than the number of its seamen or the size of its fleet, which caused Edward I to make it the 'Port' town of Chichester Harbour. In the 14th century the government reluctantly decided that there was little point in making further demands on the city for ships or seamen as it was obvious that Chichester possessed neither.

At the time of Domesday Book the population of Havant was still only around 100, compared with Chichester's 1,200 or so, but it too had achieved market town status by 1200 when the monks of Winchester Cathedral, who then owned the lordship, obtained a charter from King John. There must always have been a minor amount of pressure for trade and industry at Havant as early as 1086, for not only was the township situated at an important cross-roads but there was no demesne on which the monk's tenants could pay their dues by performing labour services. Thus from the start there would have to be rents in cash or kind, and that is the first step towards urban independence. By the 15th century, when the bishop of Winchester had taken over the lordship from the monks, a second charter was granted; this confirmed the right

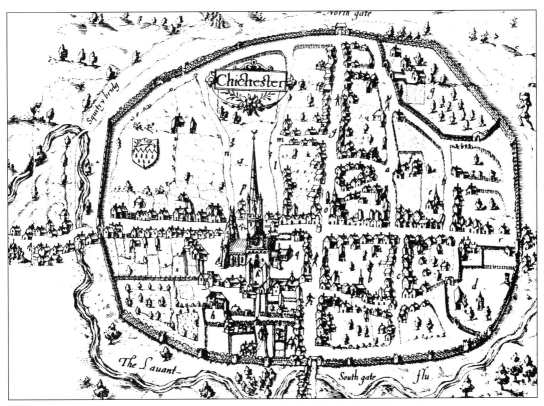

15   Chichester: the 'Port' town of Chichester Harbour. John Norden's plan of 1595 is the earliest map of the city.

to hold a market on Saturday and granted that a fair could be held 'on the Vigil and Feast of St Faith', indicating that Havant was increasing in importance as a local industrial and trading centre. In the 16th century the place was almost certainly more wealthy, probably more populous, and one suspects more important than Portsmouth in the economy of south-east Hampshire. Havant was a liberty, outside the control of the sheriff, and a peculiar, outside the normal jurisdiction of the archdeacon, which meant that its rector could grant probate, certify schoolmasters and license chirurgeons. In the returns of the Lay Subsidy for Hampshire of 1586 'The Town of Havant' paid dues of £13 9s. 8d. whilst Portsmouth Town only paid £8 7s. 4d., though if the 'Liberties of Kingston and Buckland' are added the total comes to £13 4s. 8d. Chichester's assessment in Sussex was some £45, but then its population was considerably larger.

During the course of the Middle Ages three basic industries emerged in the growing towns. Firstly came the collection and trade in wool, developing into the production of cloth; secondly came the various processes which turned hides and wool-fells into various forms of leather, vellum or parchment; finally came the buying, milling and further processing of grain, wheat and rye for bread, barley for ale and, later in malted form, for the brewing of beer. By the end of the 17th century beer had generally ceased to be something every household made for itself, but was brewed by specialists who were themselves supplied by an increasing number of maltsters.

The woollen industry in south-east Hampshire and west Sussex seems to have developed in the late 13th century from the production of homespun for local consumption. There was a

16   Havant : a clue to its past. The Homewell Spring is almost certainly the original water supply around which the earliest settlement of Havant developed.

fulling mill at Bedhampton by 1286 and by the 14th century others seem to have existed at Havant, at Broadbridge and Chichester. The Bedhampton mill was still in use in 1632, but by 1700 this and the one at Havant were grinding corn, indicating the end of the woollen industry. The presence, or absence, of fulling mills is a good indication of the state of the local industry, for they would involve a certain amount of capital outlay. Even so, in the early Middle Ages, the bulk of exports from Chichester Harbour comprised raw wool; it was only in the 15th century that at first broadcloths and later worsteds began to be exported, as will be discussed in the following chapter. The export of cloth culminated in the middle of the 16th century and then declined; the last considerable export of wool from the Port of Chichester was in 1445-6. As the Port covered a very large area at this time, not all the wool, or later, cloth, for export, could have come from the immediate area around the harbour. The export trade from Chichester was largely in the hands of native merchants. For example in 1560, of 648 cloths exported from the Port, fewer than 20 were handled by foreigners. Unfortunately the English cloth trade was subject to the whims of continental embargoes, and during the reign of Elizabeth I there were many years when no cloth was exported at all, leading to a decline in those areas which previously had depended on the export trade. By 1600 in Havant much of the cloth woven was described as being 'kersey', a light cloth used either as lining for the richer broadcloths or as the general clothing of the poor, and certainly not designed for export.

In 1616 the clothworkers of Chichester formed themselves into a guild; 11 described themselves as clothiers or dyers—the master craftsmen responsible for organising the industry—

eight were master weavers and a further eight were master fustian-weavers. There is no way of knowing how many spinners or journeymen they employed, but at that time the clothworkers were probably still the largest organised group of craftsmen in the city. The head of the guild seems to have been Thomas Miller, but when he next appears at the end of the Civil War he had become a maltster, and the cloth trade had apparently ceased.

At Havant the industry continued for a little longer, and whereas for Chichester no probate records of clothworkers survive, there are a dozen for Havant men between 1645 and 1670. When Henry Parr died in 1645 his goods and chattels were worth over £300; included in this sum were 7° 'kersies' worth £25 10s., an unspecified number 'at the weavers' worth £37 10s. and a further '6 pieces at the spinners' worth £12. He owned a dye house, dyestuffs and other materials associated with his trade. John Westbrook, another clothier who died in 1664 worth £186, also owned kersies and an amount of 'galls and copperas'—that is oak galls and the greenish crystals of ferrous sulphate, the standard agents for producing cheap black cloth. The last of the Havant clothworkers to die was probably William Mormay. He had lived in Havant since at least 1651 and died in 1669. He was a dyer with a dye-house in Homewell, but before his death he had begun to trade in malt and invest his profits in farming some land. He left goods worth £200. Included was a small amount of wood-wixen or weaver's broom, the dye plant, which may still be seen growing in Hayling Island.

The second important industry was the processing of hides and wool-fells, the latter being the skins of sheep with the wool still attached. All medieval urban economies practised the art of tanning for which a plentiful supply of water was needed; the hides needed first to be soaked in lime to remove the hair, then washed and soaked in various 'oozes' for many months. Thus when Henry Woolgar, the son-in-law of Thomas Miller, died in Chichester in 1625 he had:

> 8° dicker of upper leather in the ouze valued at £34 0s. 0d.
> 3° dicker of upper leather in the lyme valued at £10 0s. 4d.

amongst his effects. Tanning was a long-term trade which needed considerable capital as it could take as much as 18 months before the tanner saw any profit from his investment, but once this hurdle was passed then a tanner could become very rich. The most usual tanning agent throughout the period before the 19th century was oak bark which could be obtained easily from the local woodlands. The process also required the use of a lye, a mixture of potash and water. Potash was made by roasting willow twigs in iron pots. Havant still has its 'Potash Terrace' built on what was once the Potash Field where this work was carried out, and the remains of willow plantations may still be seen in the vicinity. In the past willows fringed all the local streams, their long shoots being used for basket-making.

Tanning was a smelly business, so it was usual for tanneries to be sited away from the main occupation centres as well as near to running water. At Chichester one tannery was situated outside the West Gate on the banks of the Lavant; another was at Stockbridge, south of the city. At Havant most of the tanning was carried out at Brockhampton, where there was a good supply of spring water. Here the most important of the tanning families was that of Sone; John Sone the elder died in 1668, but it was his second son, Nicholas, who took over the business. The latter died in 1689; he had married twice and fathered at least nine children, eight of whom were alive at his death. John, the second, took over the Havant tanyard, later joined by his third son, Nicholas. However the second son, Francis, being left his father's house property in Havant, sold it and moved to Chichester, buying property and land at Stockbridge where he later built a new house and managed a tanyard. Though he married twice, his daughter, Ann,

Chichester: two ancient industries that survived into the 20th century.

17 *(above) Inside the tannery of Messrs. Gibbings, Harrison and Co. at Westgate. An undated photograph showing the tanning pits and machinery.*

18 *(below) Moving a woolsack in the workshops of Ebenezer Prior, woolstaplers in Tower Street, in the 1960s.*

was the only surviving child at the time of his death in 1747 when he was a rich man and an alderman of the city.

The Stockbridge tannery seems to have gone out of production in about 1790, but that outside the West Gate lasted until well into the present century. In Havant, Thomas Land Foster was still running the tannery in Brockhampton Lane until about 1860 when the Portsmouth Water Company bought up the land around his Manor House and incorporated the springs into the water supply for Portsmouth, and later for Havant.

There are numerous mentions of fellmongers both in Chichester and Havant in the surviving records, as well as craftsmen such as glovers, saddlers and horse collar makers who worked in leather. In the 18th century there were also makers of leather breeches, such as Edward Holton of Havant who died in 1774. There are occasional references to parchment-making in Chichester in the earlier period, and parchment was obviously being made occasionally in Havant before 1790, but it was only from that date onwards that parchment-making is recorded as a specific Havant trade, and only between 1850 and 1936, when it ceased, that Havant's trade in parchment was of national significance. Even so at its most extensive only about 40 persons were employed in the Homewell parchment works.

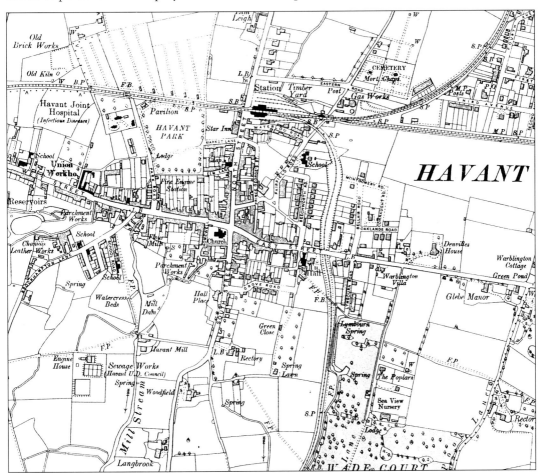

19 *Havant in 1907. The parchment works are shown on two sites south-west and west of the church. Note also the change in direction of the roadway in East Street. This still follows the re-alignment of the Roman road referred to in Chapter II. (From Ordnance Survey 6" map, surveyed 1907.)*

One specialised industry not found elsewhere in the locality was needlemaking. The industry seems to have been confined to the St Pancras district of Chichester, where the Lavant provided water and power. The trade is thought to have started in the Middle Ages as a cottage industry, was at its peak in the years before 1640, suffered seriously when the suburb was badly damaged during the Civil War and then revived in the 18th century. The last needlemaker whose name is known is James Dollman, for whom a record exists for 1788.

Following the collapse of the cloth industry, the clothiers of both Chichester and Havant seem to have turned to the making and export of malt. This industry became increasingly important after the middle of the 17th century when domestic brewing began to be supplanted by a retail trade in beer and ale. Previously small quantities of malt were made by householders producing their own 'home-brew' on a weekly basis. After the Civil War, and partly due to the increasing urban population who had no lands of their own, more and more malt was made commercially. Because malting needed space not always found in the larger urban areas, maltsters tended to be found in the smaller market towns in regions where much barley could be grown. By the 1790s some two-thirds of the total barley crop was being malted. It was particularly easy for the one-time clothier to become a maltster, as the couching house in which woad had been prepared could be converted to a malt house at little expense. Thus Thomas Miller, already referred to as a clothier in 1616, exported 23 cargoes of malt through Dell Quay in 1662, nine other maltsters also taking part in the trade. Havant, too, exported malt. In the 1650s some went to Ireland to support Cromwell's army, whilst in the 1660s more malt from Havant joined that from the Chichester maltsters in going to the West Country. By the end of the century, however, nearly all the malt exported from Chichester Harbour went to London. Maltsters, too, could become rich, and more quickly than tanners, as the process took less time and thus needed less capital to be locked away. At first the trade was thought to be dangerous as the fuel used was straw or furze, notoriously difficult to control, but greater safety and a better product came in the early 18th century when coal became the principal fuel.

Maltsters operated not only in Chichester and Havant but also at Emsworth, and in a smaller way at Bosham, the trade continuing to be very important until the end of the 19th century. Malting became an important industry due to the developing of brewing. Small breweries began to be built adjacent to local inns from the start of the 18th century; by the 19th century they were common. In 1851 there were three small breweries in Havant, two more in Emsworth. There were four of some size in Chichester at about the same time. In addition there were still a number of inns in all the local communities which brewed their own ale. Today not one remains, the last, Henty & Constable's brewery at Westgate, having closed in the mid-1950s. The 'people's beer' now comes from a handful of national breweries; to offset this a recent development has been a reversion to 18th-century practices in the form of a small number of public houses which actually brew their own ale, and very much better than the national brews it tends to be!

The populations of both Havant and Chichester increased considerably between 1670 and 1801; in 1664-5 some 900 persons lived in Havant parish, of whom over 600 lived in the town; by 1801 the population had risen to 1,670; by 1901 it had reached 3,731. In the case of Chichester, the Hearth Tax return of 1670 suggests that the then population was about 2,400; by 1801 this had increased to 4,752. In 1901, in a slightly larger area, there were almost 9,000 persons. Despite this increase Chichester was now no longer the largest town in Sussex as it had been in the reign of Charles II. In both communities the population had in fact remained fairly static in the first half of the 18th century, due to occasional epidemics in which smallpox seems to have been the greatest cause of deaths. In Chichester the worst such epidemic was that of 1722 when 168 persons died of smallpox; other serious mortality crises occurred in 1740-1,1759 and 1775. In Havant the worst years saw a smallpox outbreak in 1722-3 and a particularly bad crisis in the winter of 1746-7. The normal number of burials in Havant at this time ranged from two per month in the summer to three per month in the winter. Between October 1746 and March 1747, 46 persons died out of a population of about 800, 17 in December alone. In both cases, from about 1770 onwards, the number of baptisms began to exceed the number of burials. Following the national pattern the great surge in population had begun.

Neither Havant nor Chichester, like everywhere else in the neighbourhood of the harbour, had even the rudiments of sanitation in the middle of the 19th century when the matter became politically important. Havant set up a local health board in 1852, its first task being to examine the condition of the town and decide what should be done. A scheme to provide proper drainage was drawn up and then abandoned on the grounds of expense. Here it is worth mentioning that the provision of sewers alone could make matters worse, as it did in Emsworth in 1902 when the oyster beds were polluted.

Unlike Havant, which before 1852 had been controlled by the parish vestry which had almost no powers, Chichester had a corporation and since 1791, a board of paving commissioners which did have some powers to improve the city, not that it used them very often. When the Public Health Act of 1848 came into force and changes were the order of the day, the City Council talked a lot and did very little. Not until the mid-1870s were there piped water supplies in both Chichester and Havant. From 1880 onwards the battle in Chichester was between those who wanted drains and those who were not prepared to pay for the expense. Only at the end of the century in both communities was a modern drainage system installed.

As the 19th century progressed and the population grew larger, so, perversely, the numbers of those engaged in industry shrank whilst the numbers engaged in the service industries increased. In the 17th century there were few shops and only a limited number of persons engaged in the service of the community; most families tried to be self-sufficient. In the 19th century there were numerous shops and tradespeople providing the local inhabitants of the many small towns and urban areas with almost all their basic needs. Clothes were made locally; footwear was invariably the product of local craftsmen—boots did not even come from Northampton, let alone Italy or Brazil. There were few national chains of grocers or dairymen. Meat came from the local farms. One of the few 'imports' was the cloth used by the local tailors and dress-makers, woollens coming from Yorkshire, cottons from Lancashire. Here it is worth mentioning that the old trade in wool had recommenced in the 18th century. The produce of the Southdown flocks was collected by Chichester merchants to be forwarded to the mills of Bradford. No longer sent by sea, the merchandise went by road to London and then north by canal, and later by rail.

At the end of the present century the situation of the local communities is very different from that of even a century ago. In 1900 Havant, Emsworth and Bosham were all still recognisably different from each other and the lesser communities which surrounded them, which in some cases had changed very little since the 18th century. Chichester was different again, no longer the largest town in Sussex, it still remained the seat of a bishop, was a city with a charter and since 1889 had become a meeting place for the new West Sussex County Council. It was a place where quarter sessions were still held where lawyers lived and practised, and also the local medical centre with its hospitals and specialists. It was, however, no longer the chief town of the Port of Chichester, indeed it was no longer a real port in any sense of the word. Today all is further changed; the communities are all but merged into a part of what is called 'the Portsmouth

20   North Street, Chichester, in the late 19th century. Chichester was a thriving agricultural and market centre, although by now the water link with the harbour through Dell Quay and the Canal Basin was showing signs of decline.

Travel to Work Area'. Havant now has new industries, imported to provide work for the rising population. The last of the traditional industries, the making of gloves, ended in the 1950s. Chichester has followed a similar path and none of the industries which sustained it for a thousand years exists any longer. Even the mills which once ground corn all around the harbour are silent; milling is carried on elsewhere. Today Chichester still stands by the harbour, but it no longer lives by it, and the same is true of the majority of the harbourside communities.

IV

The Port of Chichester and the Rise of Emsworth

If nature created Chichester Harbour it was Edward I who first established the Port of Chichester in an attempt both to gain extra revenue for the Crown and to be able to keep an eye on those of his subjects too interested in 'free trade'. Edward I came to the throne in 1272 and by 1275 he had established a customs service and a dozen or so customs ports. From that time onwards duty, of one sort or another, had to be paid even if it had not always been possible to collect it in full. By 1312, when the service had been fully established, there were fewer than 15 such ports listed in the Close Rolls, with a corresponding list of their collectors. Along the south coast, from east to west, these ports were Sandwich, Winchelsea, Chichester, Southampton and Exeter, but Winchelsea, Edward's own foundation, failed to survive and Chichester's neighbour to the east became Sandwich.

In 1353 Chichester became a Staple Port, that is one officially empowered to deal with the export of wool. In 1397 the boundaries of the Port of Chichester were said to be Romney in the east and Havant in the west, and this seems to have been the pattern until the reorganisation of the 1670s. Within Chichester Harbour, Dell Quay was the only official 'port of lading' for foreign trade, but there were other minor ports in Sussex, subordinate to Chichester, and even within the harbour and its environs there were a number of authorised 'creeks' where trade could be carried on. For example, in 1335-6, of £75-worth of foreign imports landed by aliens through the Port itself, £55-worth was landed at Emsworth, the rest at Pagham.

The records which survive for the Port of Chichester indicate that from 1275 onwards the principal export was wool, and that this trade was largely handled by English merchants and exported in English-owned ships, in contrast to Sandwich where foreigners predominated. In 1279 some 500 sacks of wool were exported; a century later this had risen to almost 600, yet if we compare Chichester's exports with those of Southampton the latter port's figures are almost eight times greater. By the 16th century the principal export commodity had changed from raw wool to cloth; in 1525-6 Chichester exported some 650 broadcloths, but at Southampton it was 7,700.

The chief import was probably wine on which the king was entitled to levy tunnage, or one cask from before the mast and one cask from abaft. In 1346 Richard Marshall was appointed 'Gauger of Wines' for the two Ports of Southampton and Chichester; in the latter port both Emsworth and Bosham are named as places where wine could be landed, in addition to Chichester, which presumably meant Dell Quay. This gives some idea of the relative importance of places in the harbour.

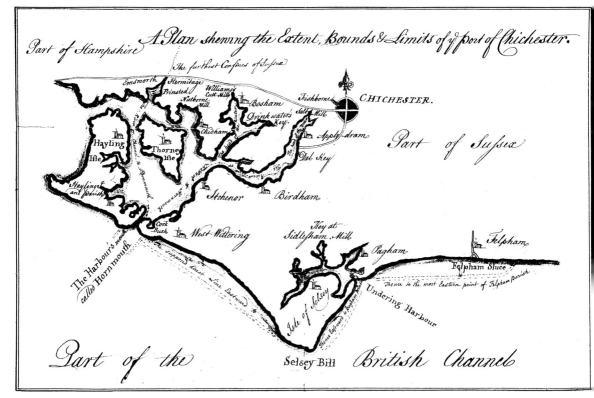

21   *Bounds of Chichester Harbour in 1680. For customs purposes the bounds of the harbour were defined as being between Hermitag*
Bridge, near Emsworth, to the most eastern part of the parish of Felpham. This map showing these bounds was drawn in the 18th century.

In addition to foreign trade, the local coastal trade was of immense importance in an age when travel by land was slow, difficult and dangerous, and travel by water far cheaper and more reliable. Indeed from the 17th century onwards the coastal trade of Chichester was the more important of the two. Of particular value was the trade to London which by Tudor times had become so large that its inhabitants could no longer be fed from its immediate vicinity. London grain merchants began to look elsewhere and the fertility of the agricultural land around Chichester Harbour attracted their attention. In 1585, in addition to a large number of barrel staves Chichester exported to London 186 quarters of wheat. (A quarter of wheat weighed roughly 500 lbs.) By 1614 this had risen to 2,330 quarters and 290 quarters of malt, and this trade in grain, malt and later flour continued to grow until in the early 18th century Daniel Defoe, in his *Tour Through the Whole Island of Great Britain*, could write:

> ... some money'd men of Chichester, Emsworth, and other places adjacent, have
> join'd their stocks together, built large granaries near the Crook ... grind and
> dress the corn, and send it to London ... by Long Sea ...

It was this trade in grain to the capital which was to make the communities around the harbour so prosperous in the 18th and early 19th centuries.

Mention has already been made of the local production of copperas for use in the dyeing trade; this too formed a part of the export trade from the Port of Chichester to London, together with other dyestuffs produced locally. Thus in 1637 Chichester sent to London 20 tons of woad and 10 tons of copperas stones, in addition to wheat and malt and hoops for barrels.

Of all the communities around the harbour, Emsworth seems to have grown and developed most rapidly, despite the fact that, unlike places such as Bosham, it seems to have had no real existence before the 12th century. Emsworth is not mentioned in Domesday Book, although some local historians have suggested that an entry which refers to a 'Newtibrigge', or Newtimber in the Hundred of Bosmere, is actually Emsworth. Newtimber, however, was elsewhere in Warblington parish, and almost certainly comprised the Wade Court/Denvilles area, as will be explained later.

It should be no surprise that the occupation of the Emsworth site occurred somewhat later than that of the other communities around the harbour, for the spring-line on which many of them stand passes to the south of the Emsworth foreshore. In the early Middle Ages both the Westbrook and the Ems were tidal and brackish, so that there was no real supply of fresh water until wells could be sunk into the chalk beneath the clay. This is not to say that no one had ever lived in the area before 1239; the Romans needed to have a ford across the Ems, and in the early 1960s traces of Saxon occupation were found in Beacon Square. The earliest reference to the name is in the mid-12th century, and it may have been

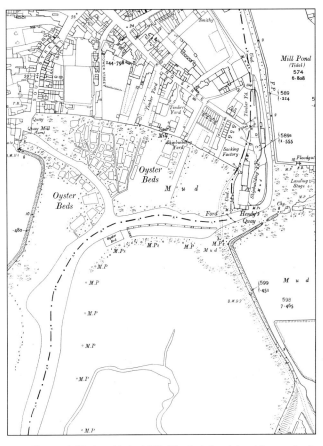

22   *Emsworth Harbourside in 1907. The dashed and dotted line marks the boundary between Hampshire and West Sussex. (From Ordnance Survey 25" map, surveyed 1907.)*

only just before this that Aemil established his 'worth', or hedged enclosure, on this site. It was probably Holinshed, in his Chronicle of 1577, who first used the term Emil—or Ems—for what was previously most likely known to the local inhabitants as the West Bourne, and said that Emsworth took its name from the river. It did not; it took its name from its first settled family and the stream was named later.

At the time of Domesday Book, Emsworth lay within the manor of Warblington; even when Emsworth became a mesne manor it lay within Warblington, the lands of both manors being intermixed. Emsworth remained in Warblington parish until the 19th century and within the civil parish of Warblington for long after that. The manor of Emsworth came into being in or around 1204, when King John gave up all hope of recovering his French lands and ordered that all his barons who held lands in both countries had to decide where they wished to live. All those who chose France forfeited their English lands which were redistributed amongst John's own followers. In 1204 the holder of the manor of Warblington was Robert de Courcy, who chose France. John gave the lordship of Warblington, with lands worth £10, to Matthew Fitzherbert, sheriff of Sussex, but he also gave £5-worth of lands within the manor to William Aquillon which was to form the mesne manor of Emsworth.

When Matthew died, his son Herbert took over the estate. Herbert had the idea that, if he could have what was in effect his own private town on his lands, he could make money. He could not ask the Crown for a fair and market at Warblington, as this was too close to the established market held by the Winchester monks at Havant, so he asked for, and obtained, a charter in 1239 which gave him the right to hold a fair at Emsworth 'on the morrow of the feast of St Thomas the Martyr' (that is St Thomas à Becket) and to hold a market every Wednesday. Emsworth is an attempt to found a town that almost succeeded, and a survey of the holdings around the Square and High Street and down South Street will show the pattern of Herbert's medieval foundation. From the late 13th century onwards Emsworth became an important 'creek' within the Port of Chichester, being mentioned frequently in the Close and Patent Rolls. In 1341 Emsworth was only one of five ports in Hampshire ordered to provide a ship to carry the new keeper of the Channel Islands and his men to their post. In 1343 Nicholas Devenish, sometime mayor of Winchester and an important wool merchant, bought the lordship of the sub-manor of Emsworth, presumably to use the place for purposes of trade. Later in the century the men of Emsworth were suspected of smuggling goods to France in spite of a royal proclamation.

Emsworth grew up not just by trade, but also because of the importance of the local fishery, both within and without the harbour. Probate records for Warblington parish in the Hampshire Record Office survive from the early 16th century until the mid-19th century. Some 160 of these refer to Emsworth people, and about a third of these are either fishermen, mariners, merchants, or those engaged in allied occupations. In the mid-17th century an Emsworth fisherman, William Spriggs, owned, amongst other goods, 'a hoy and two small boats with other fishing craft such as netts and draggs' worth £30. He no longer occupied his own home but lived with his daughter, Bridget, and her husband, John Hedger, but his household goods, clothes and money were worth £12 16s. He had money worth £33 on loan to others, and with an estate of some £76, could be thought of as being 'comfortable'.

It is impossible to say exactly how large was the population of Emsworth in the Middle Ages, but it was probably not as large as it was in the mid-17th century. In 1662 parliament voted Charles II the right to collect money on every hearth in every household in the kingdom. Lists were drawn up at intervals. The Hampshire return for 1664-5 survives in the Public Record Office, and in the three tithings which formed the parish of Warblington, some 90 households are shown. To arrive at a population estimate for communities at the time of the Hearth Tax, the accepted idea is to multiply the number of households by 4°; thus in 1664-5 the whole parish would have had a population of just over 400, of whom some 230—or 60 per cent—lived in the 52 houses in Emsworth. The other two tithings were Warblington itself, and Newtimber; in the latter there were just seven households, but the owner of the largest property was a Mr Hyde, whom it is known was the owner of the manor of Wade, so Newtimber is almost certainly the Wade Court/Denvilles area.

Earlier estimates for the population of Warblington are about 250 for 1525 and about 300 for 1603. If it is assumed that Emsworth's share was 60 per cent in both these other cases, then in 1525 the population was about 140, and in 1603 about 175, which would indicate a steady growth. A map in the British Library shows that in 1665 all the houses in Emsworth were either around the Square or in South Street. King Street and Queen Street were largely built after 1700. In 1665, with only some 50 households and rather fewer families, the community must have been very close knit, as confirmed by examining the probate records and entries in the parish register which refer to fishing families such as the Hedgers, Mansers and Holloways.

Emsworth's population increased by some 5° times between 1665 and 1811; in the latter year there were 284 houses, 329 families and a population of 1,358. As during this same period the population of England and Wales merely doubled, the economic progress made by Emsworth is clearly shown.

In the 1670s there was a general reorganisation of the system of customs ports. Under this reorganisation the western boundary of the Port of Chichester was to be Hermitage bridge and the county boundary; Emsworth was now in the Port of Portsmouth, although earlier in the century the Chichester office had maintained an agent there. Emsworth might be in the Port of Portsmouth, but Emsworth trade still had to pass down Chichester Harbour where the sole 'port of entry' in the Port of Chichester was to be Dell Quay. Emsworth had already started

23   Limits of the Port of Chichester in 1680. From an 18th-century copy of the original document.

to export corn, and this was to continue. Indeed the reorganisation may even have helped the place to grow as cargoes could go to Emsworth and did not have to go to Dell Quay. As the corn trade expanded, the men of Emsworth built a new quay on Sussex mudland, reclaimed by diverting the Ems. It could be argued that it was in both ports, or in neither. This was to be called Hendy's Quay, and it was to remain a part of Sussex until the recent change of the boundary between the two counties. When the work was done is at present unknown, but it is not unlikely that it occurred at the same time as the Hendy family built the Slipper Mill and pond some time before 1750.

Thomas Hendy, the elder, the son of William Hendy of Havant, was baptised there in 1680. In 1706 he married Ann Manser of an Emsworth fishing family. Descended both from William Spriggs and John Hedger, she had been left money by both families. By 1714 Thomas, the elder, was master of a vessel trading in grain from Emsworth to Chichester; he died in 1746. Thomas, the younger, was born in 1710. A miller and merchant, his marriage to Elizabeth Holloway made him a leading member of Emsworth society. The Holloways were an old Emsworth family recorded as fishermen as early as the 16th century. John Holloway,

Elizabeth's father, died in 1761, aged 88; he was a wealthy man and a merchant. His descend
ants would be 'gentry'.

Small fishing and trading ports need to possess adequate support services in the shape o
ship or boatyards, ropewalks, sailmakers and the like. The probate records show that at leas
two shipwrights, John Hewitt in 1607 and Isaac Hatch who died in 1618, lived in Emsworth in
the early 17th century, but neither seems to have actually worked as a shipwright there. Indeed
Hatch had probably retired to Emsworth from Portsmouth where he owned property 'on the
east side of the Point Gate', as well as two houses at Gosport. The first reference to ship
construction there seems to be in the inventory of John Smith, who died in 1700. His yard
mentioned later, was on the Westbrook, and there were to be found 'too vessels gestt bee gunn
said to be worth £15 at that stage of their construction. John had two sons, John and Robert
and a brother also called Robert, who may well have been the Robert Smith, shipwright, who
lived and had a yard at Langstone at about this time. Smith was a wealthy man: the stock o
materials in his yard was worth £160 and he also had £253 in cash. All in all, including hi
household effects, his 'goods and chattels' amounted to £480. John Smith, the younger, was
still operating this yard in 1738, but its eventual end will be discussed in a later chapter.

King Street is said to take its name from the King family. Before the late 18th century it was
known as Sweare Lane; from its southern end the Wadeway to Thorney Island commenced, the
'Sweare' being the name given to the arm of the sea which passed Emsworth on its way to Lang
stone. There had been Kings in Emsworth from at least the beginning of the 18th century. There
were others, perhaps not related, who lived at Havant and Langstone. More importantly there was
a branch at Swanwick in Titchfield parish which did have connections with the Emsworth Kings
In about 1740 and again in 1755, Kings from Titchfield came to Emsworth to marry female
cousins. They were Joseph who went to Warblington, and John who came to build ships.

When there are shipyards in a town, no matter how small, then one must expect to find
associated trades. In 1719, when Christopher Richard died, he was described as a rope-maker

24　*Emsworth fishing boats at the quayside in 1905.*

he left land at the Hermitage where his ropewalk was situated, to his daughter, Elizabeth Tanner, and her husband. By 1792 the ropewalk was owned by Richard and Stephen Miller, who were also sailmakers, as was William Preston. In 1821 Adolphus Miller at the Hermitage, and James Tatchell in King Street, are both said to have been rope-makers and sailmakers. The Tatchell family were very important to Emsworth; in 1881 the firm owned its own local transport in the form of the barge *Emsworth* of 21 tons. First registered at Portsmouth in 1864, and thought to have been built in the Emsworth shipyard, the craft remained in operation with its two-man crew until the eve of the Great War, whilst in the 1881 census Albert Tatchell was said to employ 10 men and seven boys, the largest single employer in King Street. In the 19th century almost every trade was found in Emsworth: there were tailors, boot and shoe-makers, shopkeepers selling all kinds of goods, innumerable taverns and of course the *Crown Inn* where the coaches on their way to London or the south coast towns stopped to change horses. In 1792 the licensee was John King junior who, it is said, rebuilt the frontage and changed the name from the *Three Crowns* to *The Crown*. John King's porch, with the crown on top, was unfortunately demolished in the 1960s 'in the interests of pedestrian safety'.

The coming of the Cosham-Chichester turnpike in 1762 and the opening of the canal to Arundel in 1823 did not pass Emsworth by; the former improved coach travel to a very great extent, the latter enabled barges from Emsworth to reach the centre of Chichester to the benefit of both communities.

The pattern of trade from the Port of Chichester changed during the course of the 18th century. In the years between 1660 and 1730 nearly every ship outward-bound carried a cargo

---

Harbour Shipping

The present commerce, for which customs are paid, consists of

EXPORTS - Flour to Devonshire and Cornwall.
Timber to Portsmouth and Plymouth Dock-yards.
Malt to Ireland, which trade has greatly declined.

IMPORTS - Barley from Norfolk.
Provisions from Ireland.
Coals from Newcastle.
Spanish wool and wine from Portugal.

The following is an authentic statement of the shipping in the port of Chichester since 1786, when a register was first established by act of parliament, at the interval of seven years, to 1813.

	No. of Ships	Tons	Men
1786	48	2128	143
1793	77	4085	273
1800	68	2771	186
1807	80	3043	213
1813	101	3602	337

James Dallaway, *A History of the Western Division of the County of Sussex*, vol. 1 (1815)

Harbour Cargoes, 1836

	Cargoes In	Cargoes Out
Emsworth	171	140
Bosham	4	19
Chidham	1	0
Dell Quay	113	107
Birdham	5	3
Hunston	0	1
Canal Basin	40	49
Itchenor	37	43
West Wittering	1	0
Selsey	4	0
Sidlesham	10	29
Bognor	15	1
Felpham	1	0
	402	392

John H. Farrant, *The Harbours of Sussex 1700-1914* (1976)

25 *This Emsworth public house commemorates the time when the town was the most important landing place for coal in the harbour.*

of unmilled grain; after 1730 this changed. There was less and less grain and more and more flour, mirroring the great increase in milling capacity made around the shores of the harbour from the mid-18th century onwards. In the second half of the 17th century the average annual export of grain was about 2,100 quarters (or roughly 500 tons). By 1725 this had risen to 3,600 quarters, but by 1731 less than 500 quarters of grain were shipped out compared with over 4,600 quarters of flour. In addition to flour, another important export was malt; there were traders in malt in Emsworth as well as maltsters in Havant and Chichester. Gradually, as the 18th century gave way to the 19th, the trade from Emsworth seems to have increased more than that of the other landing places in the harbour. Thus by 1836 some 40 per cent of all coastal cargoes were handled at Emsworth, compared with 28 per cent at Dell Quay, 11 per cent at the Chichester Canal Basin, and the rest elsewhere in the harbour.

Coal had been coming into the Port of Chichester from at least the mid-17th century; in 1663 John Wheeler of Emsworth, who called himself a yeoman, gave a piece of land called Coal Yard Mead to his daughter. In 1684 another Wheeler, Daniel, is listed as having some 40 tons of coal in his possession at the time of his death, and as being the owner and master of a vessel worth £80 in which he had recently made a trading voyage. In the early 19th century, when the two chief coal merchants were John Gibbs and Anthony Palmer, Emsworth was the most important landing for coal in the Port of Chichester. In 1848 when 20,000 tons came into port, half came to Emsworth, most of the rest being evenly divided between Dell Quay and the Canal Basin.

By 1848 Emsworth was at the height of its prosperity as a small Hampshire market town. It had started its own elementary school as early as 1810; St. James' Church, built in 1840, left it more independent of Warblington. Its inhabitants included doctors and lawyers as well as merchants and craftsmen. There was

26   Discharging cargo at Dell Quay in 1897. An etching by Dr Evershed of Fishbourne. Earlier in the century Dell Quay handled just over one quarter of the harbour's trade.

a bank; the Old Pharmacy, which still exists, claims to have been in business since 1812. Up to about 1850, when the railways first made their impact on the south coast, commercial traffic in Chichester Harbour increased. After that date there was a steady decline. In 1852 the customs service decided that there was no longer any point in having a customs port called Chichester—the name which had existed since the reign of Edward I was extinguished. The Sussex side became a part of the Port of Arundel, renamed Littlehampton in 1869. The Hampshire part of the harbour, finally and officially, became a part of the Port of Portsmouth. A customs post was still kept at Itchenor; today it is intermittently manned, whilst the changes brought about by the European Union mean that the old style customs duties are a thing of the past.

The decline of the coastal trade in most small ports was to be terminal, due partly to improved inland communications, in part to the increasing size of the craft which very small ports could no longer accommodate. By the mid-1920s the Canal Basin in Chichester had been shut off from the harbour because the old swing bridges had been replaced by permanent structures. Almost no trade came to Dell Quay, and commercially the harbour was all but dead. From about 1930 onwards it was only the occasional barge which reminded locals of past activities. Emsworth was slightly more fortunate. As commerce declined at the latter end of the 19th century, so long-distance fishing took its place, yet by the 1920s this too had ceased. An occasional collier still called in the years after the Great War; the last docked in 1929. As at Dell Quay, the occasional barge would call at the various landing places, but that was all. The harbour was a pleasant backwater, its peace and quiet enjoyed by the increasing number of small-boat enthusiasts. Emsworth had become a part of the Portsmouth dormitory, and few of the old skills and crafts were needed, or able, to survive.

The Western Shore – Warblington and Hayling Island

When sailing westwards up Sweare Deep from Emsworth to Langstone, the old church of Warblington is clearly visible, almost isolated at the end of its lane with only the remains of Warblington Castle, some farm buildings and a cottage for company. The castle was built in the 16th century by Lady Margaret Pole, Countess of Salisbury, on the site of the medieval manor house of Warblington and within the circuit of a Saxon moat. Slighted during the Civil War, it became the farmhouse of the Castle Farm and is today a private residence.

There were some 2,700 acres in the old parish of Warblington as it existed from medieval times to early in the present century. The southern boundary was the centre of the channel between the mainland and Hayling Island, the most northerly point was south of the Green at Rowlands Castle, and along the shore it stretched from Hermitage bridge to the Lymbourne

27   Warblington Castle. A reconstruction drawn by Richard Lally.

34

stream which divided Warblington from Havant. At the time of Domesday Book there were just 29 families in Warblington, then linked with Westbourne in Sussex, plus a further six at Newtimber, already mentioned as being the Wade Court area. This would give an estimated population of the future parish of about 150 for 1086.

The church and manor are situated where they are because of the profusion of springs there; one of them still feeds a part of the Saxon moat. To the east it is possible to trace the outline of an inlet from the harbour, at the head of which stood the mill and its pond, also spring fed. It is not certain if the church and manor were ever surrounded by a village, or whether they merely formed the 'church town' of the vill of Warblington, with the crofts and tofts of the remaining inhabitants scattered throughout the manor.

Before 1066, as part of the Westbourne holding, Warblington was a possession of the Godwin family who may well have built the original church as a private chapel to the manor house. In Saxon times the whole building was no larger than the present chancel, with the centre stage of the tower—which still survives—being the upper part of a two- storey porch from which the priest could preach to a congregation in the churchyard. When in the late 13th century a new nave was built, the upper part of this porch was kept, underpinned by the new chancel arch. When, later, the aisles were extended eastwards, this stage disappeared from view and was only re-exposed in the 1830s. In the early 14th century the old Saxon church was replaced by a new chancel and a north porch was added. The north and south arcades differ in style, possibly, so the legend runs, because the two sisters who built the nave each chose her own design. At the east end of each aisle is a late 13th-century canopied tomb, each with the effigy of a female figure and, what adds additional credence to the story, is that around 1300 there were two such sisters: Isabella Bardolf and Phyllis de Eastney, who were both associated with the manor of Warblington. The churchyard contains a splendid yew, a number of carved 18th- century tombstones and two early 19th-century flint-built sentry boxes to guard against the depredations of body-snatchers.

In the middle of the 15th century Warblington was owned by Richard Neville, Earl of Warwick, 'the Kingmaker'. He turned the fields around the church and the ruins of the manor house into a park. Later this came into the possession of Edward, Earl of War-wick, who was a better Plantagenet than Henry VII and was executed for 'trying to es-cape' from the Tower in 1499. Margaret was his sister; when Henry VIII became king he decided to create her Countess of Salisbury in her own right, to expiate Warwick's death. One of the manors which he gave her was Warblington and here, between 1513 and 1526, she built her 'castle'. Basically a fortified manor house, built four-square within the western half of the old moat and surrounded by the deer park, it was apparently a most desirable residence. After the break with Rome, which Margaret failed to support, the members of the Royal Council were worried that it was so

28 *Sentry box in Warblington churchyard. Within this isolated harbourside churchyard are two sentry boxes to guard against 19th-century body-snatchers.*

near to the open sea that messengers could easily go from it to Margaret's son, Cardinal Pole, in Rome. By a freak chance the building accounts for the year from November 1517 have survived, so we know that stone for the castle came in part from the Isle of Wight and in part from Caen in Normandy. Timber was cut in the woods of her manor of Binsted on the Isle of Wight and that, with the stone from Quarr, was shipped to Langstone, whence carts carried it to Warblington. The bricks were made on the spot, chalk came from Hambledon, slates were brought from the West Country and glass was imported from France. We even know the names of the workmen, and how much they were paid each week, from two shillings for a labourer to three shillings and eight pence for the master mason.

Margaret spared no expense. The building was just about finished by 1526, when Henry and his daughter, Mary, visited Margaret at Warblington, but by 1540 the Countess had been accused of treason, had lost her head and Henry owned the castle. It passed out of royal hands when Edward VI gave the Warblington estate to his servant, Sir Richard Cotton, and the Cottons owned the manor until the last of the line died childless in the 18th century. Sir George Cotton, who was the owner in the reign of Queen Elizabeth I, had become a Catholic under Mary, and from the 1580s onwards paid recusancy fines of £280 a year. By the 1630s the Cottons were short of money, the park became the Castle Farm and has been under cultivation ever since. In the Civil War the Cottons supported the Crown; the castle came under siege in 1643, and after capture was slighted. In the reign of Charles II the west wing became the present house, one turret of the gatehouse tower surviving, to be used as a dovecot.

In the 1660s, according to the Hearth Tax, there were some 39 households in the tithings of Warblington and Newtimber to give a population for the parish, excluding Emsworth, of about 180. By 1811 there were 61 houses in the Warblington part of the parish, containing 70 families and 299 persons, compared with 1,358 in Emsworth. At a time when the national population had doubled in 150 years, that of rural Warblington had increased by only some 60 per cent. However, the fact that there was such a small increase probably meant that on the whole individuals could prosper, and this is certainly true of those who held copyhold land at a time when the market for grain was increasing. For example, one branch of the Sone family held 50 acres of copyhold land at 'East Leigh or Stakes'-now Southleigh Farm. They paid only five shillings rent a year to the lord of the manor. When Thomas Sone died in 1673 he left possessions and money valued at about £220, a considerable sum for the time; his son John, who died in 1720, left goods, chattels and cash worth more than £1,000, over half being in money lent at interest; this is what Defoe meant when he talked about the 'money'd men of Chichester, Emsworth, and other places adjacent', engaged in the corn trade out of Chichester Harbour. Not all of the land in the manor was copyhold; much of the arable was owned by the lord and leased to farm. In the late 18th century there were four such farms: Warblington Castle Farm south of the present A259, Warblington Farm to the north of it, Mayze Coppice Farm south of Rowlands Castle, and Coldharbour Farm north of Emsworth. The former two comprised about 300 acres each and were let for a rent of about £150 a year.

Because the land of the Castle Farm had once been a park it was tithe-free at a time when tithe payments were an important part of a rector's income. When the Reverend William Norris purchased the living in 1789, he found to his disgust that the large farm facing him paid him no dues. He was so angry he even wrote to William Pitt, the prime minister, but earlier rectors had accepted a modus of £1 in lieu of tithe and successive farmers had kept the receipts. This farm had been taken over by a certain Joseph King, who had come to Emsworth from Titchfield in the mid-18th century. By 1773 he had died and his son Joseph, the second, had taken over. Joseph died young in 1788, and it was his widow Mary who had to face the rector. By her time the lease rent had risen to £180 per annum. By 1824 a new lease had been signed and the annual rent was £266 13s. 4d.; it had risen to £390 by 1858. After 1875, however, agriculture collapsed and rents dropped considerably.

Although agriculture flourished and the farmers prospered in the years after 1815, there was great hardship amongst the labourers. It was to come to a head in 1830. In 1828 Charles Osborne, who leased the Manor Farm in Hayling Island, told the members of the Parliamentary Committee on Agriculture that he had never known matters worse. The open fields had now all gone: Emsworth Common in 1810, the fields in 1819; agricultural machinery was now in use and the labourers felt that their employment was threatened. Mobs collected in the local area in November 1830; nine threshing machines were destroyed in Emsworth and Havant, but when the rioters went to Westbourne they were met by armed and mounted tenants of the Duke of Richmond supporting the magistrates and local constables. Some labourers were arrested, tried, and transported to Australia. The revolt was over.

By 1851 the population of the parish had grown to 2,302, of whom some two-thirds lived in Emsworth, and of the rest only a minority lived by agriculture. Population figures after this date mean little, for the whole parish was rapidly becoming a part of the Portsmouth dormitory; indeed, a new housing development at Denvilles, in the old Wade manor area, had started in 1890 to house both Havant and Portsmouth rather than Warblington people. By 1901 the population of Warblington had reached 3,639, the vestry had been replaced by an elected urban district council and the rector could no longer dominate the affairs of the parish as he had done over the preceding century and a half.

The story of Hayling Island is one of an isolated rural community cut off from the mainland, as the only communication was by means of the Wadeway which was under water for half of each tide, or by a ferry which would not be able to operate if the tide was running too strongly or the wind blowing too hard. A bridge was started in 1823, for reasons discussed later, but Hayling's isolation in the period before that date had a considerable effect on its development. On the other hand the soil of the island is immensely fertile. In 1086 Hayling was the most densely populated part of the harbour area with some 94 households in the 4,000 acres, giving a population of some 420, four times the number then living in Portsea.

At the time of the Conquest, William had given the greater part of Hayling Island to the monks of the abbey of Jumièges; by the early

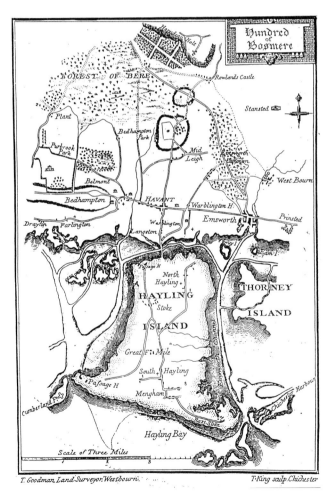

29   *Hayling Island and the mainland, 1817. Before the bridge was opened in 1824 the link with Langstone was across an ancient causeway known as the Wadeway.*

13th century they had succeeded in becoming rectors, had established a prior, who probably lived in the old manor house, and had rebuilt the chancel of St Mary's church so that he and his monks could have a suitable place of worship. Despite local opinion, there was almost certainly never a monastery as such in Hayling Island, the prior's principal task being to collect the rents and remit them to the mother house. From an account in 1294 the revenues of the priory of Hayling comprised some £80 for the rectory of Hayling, £45 for the value of the manor and about £20 from other sources, some £145 in all.

The churches of Hayling Island are St Peter's in the north, which dates from the 12th century, and St Mary's, the parish church, in the south. The oldest part of St Mary's dates from the early 13th century; the nave is somewhat later. There is a story that somewhere to the south of Hayling lie the remains of a third church, but documentary evidence does not appear to bear this out. There is considerable evidence that what was 'lost to the sea' was not a building, but land which had been part of the glebe, and that this may have occurred some time in the early 14th century. Probably this land lay within the harbour, as there was a similar land loss at Thorney Island at this time. What was certainly not lost was 'the Priory'; in the autumn of 1324 this had been seized by Edward II due to a quarrel with the French. In June 1325 the prior got his property back, and from its description, 'a messuage, garden and dove-cot', it would

30   *Hayling's link with the mainland. Hayling's isolation ended with the opening of a toll bridge for road traffic in 1824 and a railway bridge in 1867. Looking south from Langstone, this aerial view was taken in the 1920s.*

appear to have been the old manor house where the ruins of a medieval dovecot may still be seen. From the reign of Edward III until the reign of Henry V, Hayling priory was in the hands of the Crown; the last prior, one John Buket, was essentially a royal agent farming the revenue for a fixed sum and keeping the rest for himself. By 1405 he was dead, no further prior of Hayling was appointed, and in 1415 the manor of Hayling priory was given by Henry V to the new Charterhouse at Sheen.

After the Reformation, Hayling manor came into the ownership of the dukes of Norfolk, who rebuilt the manor house but seem to have left the island to its own resources because it lay 'at such a distance from the Castle of Arundel'. For this reason, in 1828, the duke sold his part of Hayling Island to William Padwick, a somewhat litigious lawyer who lived at Warblington, who had bought a considerable amount of real estate locally and planned to turn Hayling into a miniature Brighton. The proof of his dream can still be seen on Hayling Island seafront, but his scheme failed, as did his attempt to bring a railway into Hayling. He died in 1861, having quarrelled with most of those with whom he came into contact. The one good thing he did for the island was to be one of the principal sponsors of the new bridge. His name appears in the act of parliament which established the company, showing that even before he actually purchased the lordship he already had an interest in Hayling.

Hayling Bridge

The northern part of Hayling Island is united to the pleasant hamlet of Langstone ... by a handsome bridge and causeway, extending across Langstone Harbour ... The bridge is handsomely and substantially built on piles of African oak and other choice timber. It is one of the finest structures of the kind in the kingdom; it measures in length three hundred and twenty yards, and is twenty four feet wide. Its centre is composed of a swing, or swivel bridge, covering an aperture of forty feet, to admit the passage of vessels ...

The causeway, which is continuous of the bridge at each end, occupies the remaining space across the harbour ... Its sides slope diagonally, six feet horizontal to one foot perpendicular; and these slopes are faced with stone, placed at right angles, to prevent the materials washing away. The works curve slightly in a longitudinal direction, so that the road at the centre of the swing, or swivel bridge, is ten feet above the high water mark. Taking, therefore, the height at each end of the causeway, and that at the centre point of the works, it will be seen that the total ascent over the whole distance, a space of nearly twelve hundred yards, is only four feet! ...

The tolls are moderate, considering the magnitude of the undertaking, and the limited expectations that were entertained at the commencement of the works. They already produce sufficient to pay four per cent to the share-holders; and there can be but little question, from the progressive increase of visitors into the Island, that the returns will very shortly rank the undertaking amongst the most profitable in the county ...

The works were opened for public accommodation in September, 1824, with considerable *eclat*. The event was celebrated by a procession over them, of many gentlemen's carriages, and a public dinner at the Bear Inn, Havant. His Grace the Duke of Norfolk, hereditary Earl Marshal and premier peer of England, honoured both with his presence ...

Richard Scott, *A Topographical and Historical Account of Hayling Island, Hants* (1826)

If in 1086 Hayling had been the most populous place around the harbour, apart from Chichester itself, by the 16th century this was no longer the case. In 1525 there were just 72 households in Hayling, fewer than there were in 1086. In 1664-5, according to the Hearth Tax, there were 39 households in the north, and 41 in the south of the island, to give a population of some 360. By 1801 there were just 578 persons in the two parishes. In the north, which was still entirely rural, the population was 254; a century later it was 279. In the south, thanks to William Padwick and his ideas, a population of 324 in 1801 had become 1,333 in 1901. Hayling, too,

---

DIRECTORY.]   99   HEADLEY. [HANTS.]

HAYLING is an island, between the harbours of Langston and Chichester, 4 miles long, and containing 10 square miles: it comprises the parishes of North and South Hayling, in the hundred of Bosmere, union of Havant, petty sessional division of Fareham, Portsmouth county court district, diocese and archdeaconry of Winchester, and rural deanery of Havant. The island is connected with the main land by a swing bridge, erected in 1824, and repaired in 1859.

South Hayling is a parish, small watering place and village, with station on the L. B. & S. C. railway, 5 miles south from Havant, and 5 east from Southsea. The firm sands extend 5 miles, from east to west, along the shore of the English channel. The church of St. Mary the Virgin is a handsome structure, with spire and 1 bell, nave, aisles and extensive chancel, having a fine Pointed window of five arches: the crockets and finials are elaborately carved, and the font is Norman: it was restored, except the chancel, in the year 1869. The register dates from 1653. The living is a vicarage, with the perpetual curacy of North Hayling annexed, joint annual value £211, with residence, in the gift of Miss R. F. Padwick, and held by the Rev. Charles Hardy, B.A., of Christ's College, Cambridge. Here is a National school, also an Independent meeting-house. The National Life Boat Institution have a life boat here. About a mile from the church is an ancient moated encampment called Turnorbury. There was a priory here, one of the alien possessions of the Abbey of Jumieges, in Normandy: it was subsequently bestowed on the Abbey of Shene, and, at the suppression of the monasteries by Henry VIII., belonged to the College of Arundel; the dovecote is almost the only vestige remaining. The inhabitants of this island are free from all tolls, and are exempt from serving on all juries. J. C. Park, esq., is lord of the manor. The principal landowners are Frederick Padwick, esq., Capt. Lynch Staunton, and Lynch White and Thomas Harris, esqrs. The chief crops are wheat and barley. Here are Salterns, which were in existence previous to the Norman Conquest, and are mentioned in Domesday Book. The parish contains 2,582 acres, principally a strong and rich loam, and 1,779 of water; gross estimated rental, £5,464 13s. 2d.; rateable value, £4,689 2s.; the population in 1871 was 858, including 40 at coastguard station.
Parish Clerk, William King.

POST & MONEY ORDER & TELEGRAPH OFFICE & Post Office Savings Bank.— George Luff, sub-postmaster. Letters through Havant arrive at 8.15 a.m. & 3 p.m.; dispatched at 10.15 a.m. & 6 p.m.; on sunday at 10 a.m
INSURANCE AGENT.—*Phœnix & Alliance Mutual*, H. R. Trigg
National School, Wm. T. Gynes, master; Mrs. Gynes, mstrs

North Hayling is a parish and village, with station on the Hayling Island branch of the L. B. & S. C. railway, 2 miles south from Havant, 72 by road and 68 by railway from London. The church of St. Peter is a very ancient structure, with a spire containing 3 bells. The register dates from 1571. The living is annexed to South Hayling. Here is a Sunday school. J. C. Park, esq., is lord of the manor. The soil is a deep and rich loam. The chief crops are wheat, barley and oats. The parish contains 1,305 acres of strong loam, of great fertility, and 1,368 of water; gross estimated rental, £2,867 10s. 9d.; rateable value, £2,535 11s. 9d; the population in 1871 was 281.
Parish Clerk, Isaac Dibben.

———

Letters through Havant. The nearest money order office is at South Hayling

South Hayling.

Bayley Mrs. Lennox lodge
Budd Mrs. Norfolk house
Chester Mrs. Norfolk crescent
Divett George Ross, The Lodge
Fox Mrs. Staunton lodge
Hardy Rev. Charles, B.A. Vicarage
Harrison Rev. William [Independent]
Herbert Mrs. Claremont villa
Lynch Mrs. Norfolk crescent
McEuen David P. Richmond house
Padwick Misses, Manor house
Padwick Miss, Gothic cottage
Redgate J. Norfolk crescent
Ricketts Miss, Richmond terrace
Sandeman Lieut.-Col. John Glas, Westfield; & 24 Cambridge sq. London w
Sandeman Mrs. Westfield
Tompson C. W. Holly Bush cottage
Wieland Major F. Stoke lodge
Wilce James, Cupola house
Woodman George Frederick
COMMERCIAL.
Barber Edmund, baker & grocer
Barber John, shopkeeper
Beal James, chief officer of coast guard
Bevis George, farmer, Eaststoke farm
Chambers Alfred, shoe maker

Clinker George, carpenter & wheelwright, West town
Cole George, salt works
Cole James, farmer, West town
Cooper William, farmer
Crasler Jsph. Thos. farmer & landowner
Culliford Eliza (Mrs.), farmer
Cutler John, farmer, Sinah farm
Davies Henry, *Royal hotel*, & licensed to let post horses & flys
Durben John, brick maker
Francis George, painter & glazier
Goldring William, beer retailer & coxswain of life boat
Gover Willard, shoe maker
Harris Thomas, farmer & landowner
Hunt Edward, beer retailer
Jenman James, tailor & draper
Johnson Mrs. bathing establishment
Kennett William, blacksmith
Knight William, farmer, Ham farm
Luff George, grocer & postmaster
North Eliza (Mrs.), shopkeeper
North Henry, farmer, Church farm
Ogburn John, bricklayer
Pannell Lucy (Mrs.), beer retlr. West twn
Parling Heury, shoe maker
Sherman John, *Maypole*

Sims Walter, miller, Tide mill
Smith Alfred, farmer
The South of England Oyster Co. (Capt. Woods, managing director; James Dilnott, local manager)
Trigg Harry Richard, builder & surveyor & coal merchant, & agent for the lord of the manor
Vincent Jeremiah, farmer
Whicher James, butcher
Woodman George Frederick, farmer & l andowner

North Hayling.

Levett George
Turner William Carpenter, Stoke
COMMERCIAL.
Hoar Thomas, farmer
Powell Richard, farmer
Rogers David, shopkeeper
Rogers Thomas, farmer
Rogers William, blacksmith
Sims Francis, farmer
Sims Harry, farmer
Sparkes George, miller, Stoke
Thatcher Samuel, farmer, Church farm
Turner William Carpenter, farmer & landowner, Stoke

---

31 Hayling in 1875. (From Kelly's Directory of Hampshire, *1875.)*

was becoming a Portsmouth suburb, though the inhabitants would not have believed it at the time. This rise in population was largely made possible by the improvement in communications made by the 1824 bridge and the railway of 1867.

The men of Hayling, from the 18th century onwards, were chiefly engaged in agriculture. There were a few fishermen. When Walter Butler wrote his history in 1817, he listed six boats from North Hayling and 12 from 'Sinar' working the western harbour. Hayling's principal landing place was near the tide mill in the centre of the eastern side of the island, whence barges took corn to Chichester, and brought in coal, chalk and manure. The trade had virtually ceased by 1939, but there is still a requirement on the owner of the adjacent land to maintain this quay should it ever be required again.

There has never been a village centre in Hayling Island, a point emphasised by Richard Scott in his history of 1826. He suggested that the scattered dwellings had been there since the time of the first Saxon settlers. A careful study of the houses on Hayling today would reveal that many, if not most, of those existing in the early 19th century have managed to survive the hands of developers.

During the last century, whilst the population of South Hayling has increased, the north is still largely rural; one hopes that it will remain so as the local soil is amongst the most fertile in the country. Even in an age of butter mountains and wine lakes it is as well not to destroy too much of the countryside by covering it with bricks and mortar, one of the fundamental policies advocated by the Chichester Harbour Conservancy. Even after 1875 grain was still being grown at a profit and exported from Hayling. Sheep were grazed on the saltings in summer, and wintered on the fallow. Salt-making and brick-making continued, the former until the late 19th century, the latter to this day. Whilst almost all the land in the south had been enclosed before

32   Langstone-Hayling toll bridge in 1933.

1800, land in the north was still farmed communally as open fields as late as 1837, largely because a minority of the tenants belonged to the manor of Havant. In 1840 acts of enclosure for the common fields were passed, and by 1876, apart from the Beachlands, all the Hayling Island commons had also been enclosed. The old order had changed and Hayling had finally left the Middle Ages behind.

Hayling Island Salt

The principal branch of trade carried on in the Island is that of making salt. There is a very fine salt-work in the north, and another in the south parish; and there are three others in the Island. Mention is made of a saltern in Hayling, (probably that in the north) so early as in the reign of William the First. It is therefore apparent that Salt was the staple article of manufacture in the island long before the Conquest. The salt made here is of excellent quality, and is generally preferred to any other. St. Augustin ... speaks in strong terms of the salt made round its shores, and says that it is superior to every other made on the British coasts.

Richard Scott, *A Topographical and Historical Account of Hayling Island, Hants* (1826)

VI

The Port of Langstone and the Chichester Canal

Langstone was the port for Havant; it was never very large and could only accommodate small vessels until the completion of the bridge to Hayling Island in 1824. Situated at the head of both Chichester and Langstone Harbours, it could be approached from either direction. In the Middle Ages it marked the western limit of the Port of Chichester. The ancient Wadeway to Hayling Island, which started at the eastern end of Langstone High Street, followed the natural watershed between the two harbours: all streams entering the waters to the west of the Wadeway flow into Langstone, all streams to the east into Chichester Harbour. The name Langstone comes from 'the place of the Long Stone'; it is not 'Lang's Ton' as has been suggested. Both 'Langstone' and 'Langston' have been used in the past, but it is now generally held that the former is correct.

There are references to Langstone as a port in the medieval records, but as a port the place can never have amounted to much. Like Chichester Harbour, that of Langstone was difficult to enter because of a bar, which at low-

33   The Wadeway at Langstone in 1987. For many centuries this ancient track was the only route—other than by boat—between the mainland and Hayling Island. The track has deteriorated and can be extremely dangerous to follow.

water spring tides had only a foot or two of water over it. In 1817 Walter Butler said that the hamlet comprised three mills, 12 houses and an inn. From the earliest times the inn would have been needed as a halting place for travellers waiting to cross the Wadeway to Hayling Island. In 1678 the widow Elizabeth Gibbons of Langstone died, owed some £10 by the government for payment for soldiers billeted on her, and so she must have been the Langstone inn-keeper. In 1678, too, died James King of Langstone, mariner, who owned half a share in the ketch *Elizabeth of Langstone*, worth £59. He also owned a hoy and two boats worth a further £60. His widow remarried a certain Robert Smith, shipwright of Langstone, who was probably the brother of

AN

A C T

FOR

Making and maintaining a Navigable Canal from
the River Arun to Chichester Harbour, and from
thence to Langstone, and Portsmouth Harbours,
with a Cut or Branch from Hunston Common,
to or near the City of Chichester, and for
improving the Navigation of the Harbour of
Langstone, and Channels of Langstone, and
Thorney.

[Royal Assent, July 7, 1817.]

WHEREAS the making and maintaining a canal, naviga- Preamble.
ble for boats, barges, and other vessels from the river
Arun, at or near to a certain public house, called the Ship
and Anchor, in the parish of Ford in the county of Sussex to
the harbour of Chichester, at or near to a certain place called
the Salterns in the parishes of Birdham and Itchenor in the
said county of Sussex, in, to, or through the several parishes of
Ford, Yapton, Barnham, Aldingbourn, Birsted, Oving, Mer-
ston, North Mundham, Hunston, Donnington, Appledram,
Birdham and Itchenor, or some or one of them in the said
county of Sussex: And also the making and maintaining
No. 1.   A

34   Canal navigation through Chichester Harbour. Part of the preamble to the Act of 1817.

John Smith, the contemporary Emsworth ship-builder, in whose will, proved in September 1700, a Robert Smith was named as a trustee.

By the end of the 18th century some half a dozen small sloops were said to use the port of Langstone, mostly using the Langstone approach. They brought in coal from Sunderland and took out grain, malt, flour and probably some salt from the North Hayling saltern at the head of Sweare Deep. Then in 1817 everything changed. The Portsmouth and Arundel Canal Company was formed, with powers to construct a channel between Langstone and Chichester Harbours. By 1820 the so-called 'New Cut' had breached the Wadeway and in consequence a bridge would have to be built. By the 1817 Act it was originally intended that this 'restoration of a right of way' would be carried out by the canal company itself; instead a new company was set up by the local worthies of Havant and Hayling to build a toll bridge to Hayling Island. Their Act received royal assent in May 1823 and included the right to construct wharves and 'wharehouses' at Langstone. £12,000 could be raised by shares, and the canal company paid over the sum of £3,580 which was thought to be the cost of 'bridging the Wadeway'. Once the new quays, wharves and warehouse had been built, Langstone became a port which could accept much larger vessels, and the approach from Chichester Harbour was greatly improved. This was one of the more unexpected developments of the construction of the Portsmouth—Arundel Canal, and somewhat more successful.

The Canal Age in Great Britain was started in the 1760s when the Duke of Bridgewater, aided by James Brindley his engineer, built the Worsley Canal to bring coals to Manchester. By 1800 the basic pattern of the new inland waterway system had been completed. The river systems of the north-west and north-east were now connected to those of East Anglia and there were also links with the Severn river system and the Thames. Then during the Napoleonic wars there were proposals to link Portsmouth with London to cut out the long beat up the Channel and avoid the French privateers clustered around Dunkirk. An inland voyage would also avoid bad weather in the Channel; if the wind was unfavourable it might take a week to sail from Portsmouth to the Downs, and almost as long from there to the London docks. The parliamentary bill that emerged in 1815 planned to link Portsmouth—through Chichester Harbour—to the Arun, whence barges could then travel north through the Wey and Arun Canal to the Thames and London.

As early as the reign of Queen Elizabeth I it had been suggested that a canal needed to be built from Fishbourne creek to the heart of Chichester, but nothing came of it. In 1801 this idea was revived and in both that year and again in 1811 there were proposals to create short

35   The New Cut. Made for the harbour navigation in about 1820. This deepening of the channel breached the Hayling-Langstone causeway - the Wadeway - creating the need for a road bridge built a few years later.

'cuts' from the harbour to the city; neither scheme came to anything. More adventurous was John Rennie's plan of 1803. Starting at Flathouse Quay in Portsea, the canal would have crossed Portscreek, near the old bridge, passed south of Cosham, Farlington and Havant, and then looped to the north of Emsworth before following the northern shore of the harbour. The navigation would then pass to the south of Chichester, and from Mundham follow the line eventually constructed by the Arundel Canal. In both 1803 and again in 1810 parliament rejected the plan, but by 1815 there were two new developments. Firstly came the impending opening of the Wey and Arun Canal, and secondly steam-driven tugs had arrived: there would be no need to make a 'cut' all the way through the farmland south of Portsdown Hill, as tugs could tow the barges from locks at Milton through the harbours to further locks on the Birdham shore. A new plan was drawn up in 1815, and the Act establishing the canal company received

36   Salterns Lock, Birdham, in about 1910. Through this sea-lock the canal links with the harbour. Opened in 1823, barges from the harbour could navigate from here to Chichester or to the river Arun at Ford and thence to the waterway system throughout the country.

Chichester Harbour Canal Link

The Canal which is now under execution, to form a junction between the Rivers Wey and Arun, will open a communication between London and Arundel ... but owing to the uncertainty of a Coasting Voyage from Arundel to Portsmouth; and the loss, detention, and inconvenience which attends the shifting of Cargoes, the transit of Goods between London and Portsmouth cannot be at all calculated on, while a distance, of at least thirty miles is to be performed by Sea; and therefore, the benefits of a thorough Trade of an Inland Navigation ... will in a great measure be lost, unless it is continued on from Arundel to Portsmouth ...

The line, now surveyed, departs from the River Arun at Ford ... from thence it takes a direction by the south of Yapton and Barnham to Lidsey, and through Colworth, Runcton, and Donnington, to the Harbour of Chichester, descending into the Tideway at the Salterns in the Parish of Birdham ...

The Navigation from Chichester Harbour is proposed to be made in the Tideway by the Channel north of Thorney Island, and that north of Hayling Island, into Langston Harbour ... The Channel of Langston Harbour is deep to ... Eastney Lake, which departs from the Harbour at the point north of Cumberland Fort, where the Ferry to Hayling Island now is. The Channel of Eastney Lake is deep to near the Convict Watering Place. From this Lake therefore I advise a line of Canal to be made across Portsea Island, to the Halfway Houses in Portsea Common, a central point between the Towns of Portsmouth and Portsea ...

It is proposed to make another Cut between Portsmouth Harbour and Langston Harbour, by Wymmering ...

Goods may be sent from London, and proceed without interruption to Portsmouth. The Barges will be towed by horses until they reach Chichester Harbour, and from thence to the Line of Portsea, in the Tide-way by Steam-boats ...

Instead, therefore, of goods being sent Coast-ways between London and Portsmouth, Havant, Emsworth, Chichester, or Arundel, there can be no doubt, that they will be sent by this Line of Canal. Naval and Military stores will likewise form great articles of trade, as well as East and West India goods, particularly in the time of War; and when to these the local trade is added, I think it cannot fail to give an ample return for the money it is likely to cost.

John Rennie, *A Report to the Subscribers to a Canal from Arundel to Portsmouth* (1816)

royal assent in July 1817; the company was now in business. The proposed canal would have four sections: the first through Portsea Island from the Halfway Houses—roughly the site of Portsmouth and Southsea railway station, hence Arundel Street—to Milton Lock; the second through the harbours, cutting the Hayling Wadeway; the third from Salterns Lock to Hunston Common, from which point a branch went north to the Canal Basin dug south of Chichester; the fourth section went from Hunston to join the Arun at Ford. In 1818 work began both at Ford, and in Portsea Island. The Act had given the proprietors of the canal the right to raise capital of £126,000. Much of this money was raised locally by the sale of £50 shares, but this sum proved to be insufficient and by 1824 a further £40,000 was raised in the form of a loan from the government, justified by the fact that the canal company was 'setting the poor to work' in an age of increasing rural unemployment.

The Portsmouth-Arundel Canal was officially opened in May 1823, although the Portsmouth sections had been ready for navigation since the previous autumn. The company's steam tug was called the *Egremont*, after the 3rd Earl of Egremont of Petworth House, a leading protagonist in the building of the canal and one of the principal shareholders. On the day of opening her master distinguished himself by stranding his vessel and her string of barges on a sandbank in the harbour and arriving late for the ceremony, but subsequent trips between the two locks seem to have been uneventful. Barges brought to Salterns Locks in this way were then towed by horse to the Canal Basin, or else on from Hunston to Ford.

By 1827 it had become apparent that the 'cut' through Portsea Island to Milton was a mistake. Salt water was contaminating the local wells and alternative arrangements had to be found. An additional Act was passed in May 1828 which allowed the company to raise further capital 'not exceeding £50,000' to widen Portscreek, and to start its Portsmouth operation at Flathouse Quay, paying to Portsmouth Corporation the usual wharfage dues. This new departure seems to have succeeded in improving the company's fortunes. In 1830, for example, 'about twenty tons of marble ex *Asia* 84 [guns] for His Majesty at Windsor and above forty tons of gold and silver for the Bank of England' were, with other goods, sent from Portsmouth to London in one week. The traffic did not last. By 1838 the Portsea Island section of the canal had been abandoned. By 1855 the section between Ford and Hunston was in disuse; only the section between Salterns Lock and the Canal Basin at Chichester was actually working. After about 1845 the goods chiefly landed here were coal, timber, lime, sand and gravel. As mentioned earlier, in 1851 one quarter of the coal entering the harbour went to the Canal Basin. By the 1880s most goods destined for Chichester were unloaded into barges off Itchenor and were then carried to the Canal Basin. In 1886 it was reported that of 471 vessels entering the harbour only 21 were unloaded in Chichester, and they were barges.

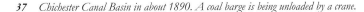

37   Chichester Canal Basin in about 1890. A coal barge is being unloaded by a crane.

CHICHESTER CANAL.

CLASSIFICATION OF MERCHANDISE

FOR THE WHOLE OR ANY PART OF THE CANAL.

MERCHANDISE.	Amounts payable in respect thereof including use of Wharf for a reasonable period.
Sand	6d. per ton.
Coal	6d. „
Timber	9d. „
Slates	6d. „
Bricks	6d. „
Iron	6d. „
Manure	6d. „
Shingle	6d. „
Gas Water in Barrels	6d. „
Tar	6d. „
Coke	6d. „
All other Goods	6d. „

1st January, 1895.

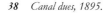

38   *Canal dues, 1895.*

39   *The sailing barge* Fanny. *The view is at Hunston and the barge is bound for Chichester Canal Basin in about 1909.*

Barges were still coming to the Canal Basin before the First World War, but by 1924-5 the road crossings at Donnington and Birdham had been filled in and the Canal Basin was effectively sealed off from the harbour.

The reasons for the rapid decline of the Portsmouth—Arundel Canal were, firstly that it was no longer necessary for a sailing vessel to 'beat up the channel', as a tug would be waiting off Dungeness to provide a fast passage to London Docks; secondly, there was the development of the railway system. The London, Brighton and South Coast Railway had reached Chichester by 1846; the line passed through Havant later in the same year and had reached Portsmouth by 1847, its passage from Fratton to Commercial Road made easier by the acquisition of the old bed of the canal. The amount of goods carried on the canal from Birdham to the Basin between 1868 and 1898 declined, from 7,070 tons to 704 tons. In 1892 the assets of the canal company had been transferred to Chichester Corporation. The Canal Age was over.

At the other end of the harbour the canal and bridge companies combined to bring new life to Langstone. It was now said that vessels of up to 400 tons could berth at the quays there, although there is little evidence that any vessels as large as that actually did so. Most of the

40   *Chichester Canal Basin in the 1920s. This photograph, taken from an aerial balloon, shows the wharves of David Cover and Son, timber merchants, and coal supplies for the Chichester Gas Company.*

cargo reaching Langstone seems, as heretofore, to have come in very small coastal vessels or barges. When the railway first came to Havant the bridge company began to think in terms of building a connecting spur from Langstone to Havant. The idea was abandoned, but from 1860 onwards a line was constructed as part of a much larger design, a railway to Hayling Island itself. The line was open as far as Langstone Wharf by 1864. The line to South Hayling over the viaduct with its swing bridge had been completed by 1867, and the London, Brighton and South Coast Railway took over the running both of the railway, the bridge and the wharves at Langstone, although the Hayling Railway Company was nominally independent until the Railway Grouping Act took effect in 1923.

The Langstone wharves were not great money spinners but, during most of the period from the 1870s to the Great War, a constant stream of small coasting vessels came to Langstone from Plymouth with cargoes of fertilizer which were taken by rail as far away as Pulborough and Horsham. During this period, too, the wharves and bridge tolls were leased to the Little family of Havant who managed a number of barges of their own, engaged in the trade of sand and gravel, and in any other cargo they could find.

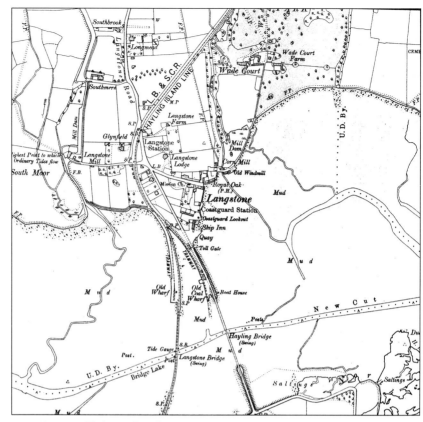

41   Langstone Harbour and its wharves in 1906. (From Ordnance Survey 6" map, surveyed 1906.)

42   Langstone Harbour earlier this century. To the left of Langstone Quay is the Ship Inn, *and to the right the* Royal Oak.

For a short time in the 1880s there was even a train ferry from Langstone Wharf to Brading Harbour with the coaches and wagons carried on a small double-ended vessel, but the experiment only lasted for a few years, and has more to do with Langstone than Chichester Harbour.

The Little family's barges and other similar vessels were small, flat-bottomed, and around 20 tons in burden. They worked both the Chichester and Langstone Harbours and could carry some 15-20 tons of sand or gravel, dredged from the harbours or from the banks outside them. Occasionally they could be used to take cargoes of grain as far afield as Southampton, but most of their work was local. There are the remains of three or four of these barges still to be seen locally. One, the *Langstone*, was built in 1900 by Albert Apps of Emsworth for Mrs Jane Little, then managing the company. The vessel was of 20-registered tons and rigged as a gaff-ketch but was given a motor in the 1920s. She finished working in about 1940. Another of the Littles' craft was the *Gladys*, also built by Apps at Emsworth in 1894 and also of 20 tons. Unlike the *Langstone* she had a rounded bottom and a higher freeboard and was thus less suitable for 'sitting on the bank' where the crew would dig what was needed, running the sand or gravel up a plank in a wheelbarrow before tipping it into the hold. The log of the *Albert* for 1894 has survived; her master was Ernest Churcher, and the most common entry is 'down Chichester Harbour for Gravil'. His other entries also tend to have his own rather original spelling! The Langstone barges as a whole operated under sail up to about 1920 when motors began to be installed, and by about 1930 almost all were so fitted, whilst still using sail if required. They had no lee-boards and were not considered sufficiently seaworthy to venture outside the protected waters of the Solent and Spithead, but served a most useful purpose. Similar barges were also found at Emsworth, owned by both J.D. Foster and John Kennett. Today no cargoes come to Langstone, as elsewhere in the harbour, but the remains of the *Langstone* may still be seen off Langstone Mill.

43   *Wreck of the* Langstone *barge. Photographed off Langstone Mill at low tide, November 1995.*

VII

The Hundred, Manor, Parish and Village of Bosham

With over 3,000 acres the parish of Bosham was the largest on the Sussex shore of the harbour by the 14th century, but at the time of the Conquest the manor of Bosham was far larger as it included the whole of Funtington, the Ashlings, West Stoke and Apuldram, with some additional lands at Itchenor and Birdham. Domesday Book records some 90 peasant families in Bosham manor itself, which means that, including 17 'servi' (serfs), between 400 and 450 persons lived on the estate. Because Bosham had been the favourite home of the Godwins in 1066, 11 'hawes'—perhaps market stalls, perhaps actual houses—in Chichester belonged to the lord of Bosham, but all but one had been given to the bishop by William, presumably when the cathedral moved there from Selsey. On the manor there were no fewer than eight mills, indicating how great the production of corn must have been, not surprising given the great fertility of the soil in the Bosham area. On the other hand, and again surprisingly, knowing the richness of the harbour, the fisheries were worth very little. Lastly there is mention of woodland where swine could be pastured; a modern remnant is Old Park Wood, but in 1086 there were other woods inland around the Ashlings which were also swine pastures.

The greater part of the soil of the Bosham peninsula is brickearth lying over chalk; extremely fertile, it explains the presence of the Roman settlement at Broadbridge. In the north of the parish, where the chalk subsoil emerges from beneath the Reading Clay, is a line of springs, as at Old Fishbourne and Broadbridge. To the south of this line springs do not exist, but ample supplies of water can usually be obtained from shallow wells sunk through the brickearth into the chalk.

In this peninsula there is not a natural watercourse sufficiently powerful to drive a mill or to provide water in time of drought. The Bosham Brook, now more frequently called the Mill-stream, is not a natural watercourse but artificial, as study both of its present course and the geological survey map clearly shows. The headwaters of the brook rise from the springs at Funtington; the streams unite near West Ashling Mill, flow south past Ratham and on to Broadbridge, both sites of mills. From Broadbridge the geological survey shows the brook entering the north-east corner of Bosham Creek. At some time in the past—and it has been suggested that if the Quay Mill did exist at the time of Domesday then this date must be before 1086 and could even have been in Roman times—a leat was dug from just south of Ratham to Bosham, but the channel which exists today along Ratham Lane seems more likely to date from the 18th century than from an earlier time.

44   Quay Mill, Bosham, in 1902.

There were originally seven tithings in the parish of Bosham: the first was the village itself around its church; a second was Broadbridge, the area around the modern railway station and the Swan cross-roads; the third, Old Fishbourne, lay either side of the present A259 with its western border roughly halfway between the *Swan* and the *Black Boy* and its eastern boundary formed by Salthill Road to the north and Fishbourne Creek to the south; Creed was centred on the present school and village hall; Walton lay towards the southern end of Walton Lane; Hook and Southwood, in the south of the parish, are today marked by farms. In the 19th century the area to the south of Bosham on the other side of the water was called Gosport, that name replacing Southwood as one of the tithings in the 19th-century census returns.

Any population figures for the parish of Bosham must include all the tithings, so although an approximate figure can be calculated for the population of the village itself, this will not necessarily be the same as the figure given for the parish as a whole.

By the accident that Harold Godwinson had made himself king on the death of Edward the Confessor, and then had fallen at Hastings, William seized the lordship and kept the manor as part of his royal demesne, the only such holding he kept in Sussex. During the course of the Middle Ages Bosham was granted to various noblemen, brought back into the hands of the Crown and then regranted, until at the end of the 15th century it became a possession of the Berkeley family; the direct line held the estate until 1810 when the then earl granted Bosham to the cadet branch of the barons Hardinge, who in turn passed the land to the barons Gifford. The family finally left Bosham when the estate was sold in 1918. In the 1920s the manor was acquired by the first Earl of Iveagh. It is now a part of the family trust and is managed on its behalf by the Manor of Bosham Ltd. The only reminder of the Berkeley connection is the public house called the *Berkeley Arms* at the southern end of Delling Lane.

Because the manor was technically 'ancient demesne of the Crown', the inhabitants had certain rights, as did those on all ancient demesne, but Bosham seems to be unique in keeping

Men of Bosham

Men of Bosham claim rights in Chichester Harbour - and beyond - based on generations of forebears who made their living from the sea. Their claims, enshrined in centuries-old documents, have led to complex legal disputes in more recent history.

In the 1930s Chichester Corporation promoted legislation to empower the city to collect tolls, rents and dues within the Sussex side of the harbour. The Men of Bosham were in open revolt, opposing the parliamentary bill on the grounds that they would be deprived of their ancient rights of free moorings, free wildfowling and free fishing. As 'men and tenants' of Bosham Manor—a manor 'of ancient demesne of the Crown'—they had been granted freedom from tolls throughout the realm from time immemorial. They won the day when a special section was inserted into the Chichester Harbour Act of 1938 protecting these rights: nothing should prejudice any right, privilege or exemption conferred on the Men of Bosham by royal charter granted by James I as confirmation of ancient custom 'from the time whereof the Memory of Man is not to the contrary'. Part of this early 17th-century Bosham Charter commanded that

> Men and Tenants of the Manor of Bosham
> ... be exempt from Homage or Payment of
> Tolls ... throughout our ... Realm.

In 1960 the case of Edwin Martin, Man of Bosham, went to the High Court when he contested the right of Lord Iveagh, Lord of the Manor of Bosham, to charge him for 'mooring boats to the quay and piles at Bosham'. He claimed that as long ago as Richard II's reign in 1388 there was a reference to the Men of Bosham when 'all the men and tenants ... of the manor of Bosham ... [were] to be quit of payment of toll ...'

Martin's claim to be a Man of Bosham was upheld as was his right to moor free of charge as long as his boat was used primarily for fishing: he could use the quay at Bosham without payment for getting to and from his boat or unloading fish. But the High Court judgment made him liable to pay the mooring charge of £48 19s.6d. claimed by Lord Iveagh on the technicality that at the material time the boat in question was being used as his houseboat and the owner could not claim to be living on land within the Manor of Bosham.

Today, Simon Combes, the youngest Man of Bosham, and one of the last, claims rights in the harbour which are honoured by the Chichester Harbour Conservancy.

Kim Leslie

them, as various rulers have confirmed the rights by charter, the last being given to 'the Men of Bosham' by James I. Because of the long and continuous connection with the Berkeley family, who in addition to being lords of the manor also claimed the right to hold the view of frankpledge within the hundred of Bosham, the estate remained feudal for longer than any other on the shores of the harbour. Frankpledge was the system started by the Saxon kings by which every adult male was sworn into a tithing to 'keep the king's peace'; normally this duty in the Middle Ages belonged to the sheriff. It was on this occasion that the tithingmen and constables were elected, but not in Bosham, Funtington, the Ashlings or Thorney Island. Long after elections of these officers had passed to the parishes, to be approved by the justices, the lords of the manor of Bosham held their hundred court and appointed those officials themselves. In the 1850s when county police forces were established, the habit of electing parish constables and tithingmen ceased, and they no longer had any powers, yet the hundred court of Bosham still met formally until the eve of the Great War. The sinecure offices were filled, but the holders were then dined, the last flourish of an ancient tradition.

As in every manor there were a number of lesser estates held by men who had been granted their land directly by the Crown or earlier lords. These freeholders usually had to provide a service on certain named occasions. One such existed at Broadbridge in Bosham. In the mid-13th century the landholder was a certain William Papillon; his service was to provide the king with two white capons whenever the monarch passed through Bosham. On 9 August 1269 when Henry III passed by on his way from Chichester to Winchester he duly demanded, and received, his due. By 1545 the holding had been divided, so when Ellis Bradshawe died in that year he was said to hold 'a toft, a fulling mill and land at Broadbridge by service of one white capon' whenever the king came to claim it.

In 1301 Edward I granted the manor of Bosham to the Earl of Norfolk for life. However, a few years later Edward II seems to have decided that he still had rights over the woodland, so he ordered the sheriff of Sussex to fell all dead wood and unfit timber in his wood at Bosham, to make 100 quarters of charcoal and to take it to Boulogne to be delivered to the king's scullion there. This information comes from the Close Roll; another entry, this time from the Patent Roll, suggests that long before they held the manor, the Berkeleys had an interest there. In September 1327 Peter de Berkele, king's clerk, was granted a prebend at Bosham formerly held by Master James de Berkele, deceased, which must bring us to the church at Bosham and its college.

45 Bosham church and Quay Meadow in 1903. The harbourside church is one of the oldest Christian sites in Sussex.

The church of the Holy Trinity, Bosham, is one of the oldest Christian sites in Sussex; according to Bede, the Irish monk Dicul had a cell here even before St Wilfred arrived. The oldest part of the present structure, the lower part of the tower, is thought to date from the late 9th century. Then, in the first half of the 11th century, Earl Godwin rebuilt the church. His building was large for a Saxon church of the time, showing the importance of Bosham and its lords in the years before the Conquest. From this period date the chancel arch, which appears on the Bayeux Tapestry, and the western arch beneath the tower. The late Saxon nave probably had no aisles, and the chancel was much shorter than the one which exists today. The latter was lengthened twice, first in the 12th century and again in the 13th, at which time the north and south aisles were added and the walls of the Saxon nave were pierced to form the present arcades. The spire was added in the 14th century and the south porch in the 16th and 17th centuries. The original high-pitched roof was replaced by a much flatter one in the 15th century and restored to its original height in 1865. There is a small crypt beneath the south aisle which some have suggested might have been the original cell of Dicul, but almost certainly was not.

There is a story that a daughter of Canute was drowned in the millstream and buried in Bosham church; in 1865 the site of the supposed tomb was excavated and the remains of a female child were found. The then vicar felt that this confirmed the story of the Danish princess, but modern local historians disagree, for there is no evidence whatsoever that Canute ever had a palace here, nor is there evidence that a daughter of his died young.

During the reign of the Confessor the advowson of the church at Bosham, with all the lands it owned, was granted to his own chaplain, Osbern, whom William later made bishop of Exeter. Some of the church's possessions, such as Chidham and Thorney, were local, but others such as Plumpton and Saddlescombe were quite a distance away. The seat of this manor came to be Chidham. Much to the chagrin of the bishop of Chichester, Bosham church and its estates came under the jurisdiction of the diocese of Exeter. There were a number of quarrels between the prelates concerning this, and in 1327 the bishop of Chichester managed to get a statement from the Crown that although Bosham did belong to the Exeter diocese he had the right of visitation, and his fellow bishop had to accept this.

Some time in the reign of Henry I the bishop of Exeter established a college of secular canons at Bosham; the bishop himself was dean of the college, but he would obviously be non-resident. There were six prebends for the six canons, but only one, the sacristan, needed to be permanently in residence. The six were Bosham Parochial, Walton, Funtington, Apuldram, Chidham and Westbrooke. The canons were endowed with the great tithes in their prebends and such lands as were owned by the church. Each had to appoint a vicar to carry out his parochial work in his prebend because five of them would be likely to be resident elsewhere—at one time the prebend of Apuldram was held by no less a person than William of Wykeham, bishop of Winchester. As absentees they tended to neglect Bosham and failed to keep the vicars under proper supervision. There were constant complaints, solved to some extent when the vicars were made to live in a house built to the south of the present church. A medieval gateway in the wall to the south of the path leading to Quay Meadow is said to mark the site. In 1548 the college was dissolved, the prebendaries pensioned off and the parochial vicar became the vicar of Bosham.

The building now called the Manor House, immediately to the north of the churchyard, is almost certainly on the site of the original Saxon and medieval manors. To the east is a small moated area said to have been the site of the original house. The present building is largely the work of the Berkeleys and dates from the 17th and 18th centuries, but there is medieval work from the 12th or 13th centuries at the back. In a survey of 1801 the occupier was a Mrs Bennett who farmed the local land, but it was still called the Manor House, and various 19th-century directories also follow that practice. The Fitzhardinges, as lords of the manor, lived at Old Park in Old Fishbourne.

Statistics to help assess the population both of Bosham village and the tithings are scarce. In the Sussex subsidy for 1296 there are 61 names for five of the tithings, but Bosham is not included; in 1327, 75 names are mentioned. By then both Funtington and Apuldram had ceased to be a part of the manor, so it looks as if in the mid-14th century as many people were living in half the area as had lived in 'Greater Bosham' in 1086, that is some 300 to 400 persons. The 17th-century Hearth Tax returns can usually be relied on to give fairly accurate assessments of the numbers of households in every tithing; unfortunately many of the returns for Bosham parish are so badly rubbed as to be impossible to decipher. An alternative source for the 17th century is Archbishop Compton's census of 1676. This should give an exact total of all the adult communicants, non-conformists and catholics in a parish, but the vicar of Bosham merely gave an approximation: his return said that there were 300 communicants, which should mean about 500 persons to the nearest round score, but the Hearth Tax returns for both Broadbridge and Southwood are legible, and suggest that about 100 persons lived in those tithings. If we assume that at least as many lived in the other three tithings, then the population of Bosham village in the second half of the 17th century would have been about 300, making the settlement slightly larger than that at Emsworth.

Study of the baptismal and burial registers of Bosham for the whole of the 18th century indicates that not until after about 1760 was the population likely to have increased. There were serious epidemics, probably of smallpox, in 1720-1, 1731, and 1740-1. On the latter occasion the vicar noted that 16 smallpox cases had been buried. There was a further epidemic in 1780-1, when burials were 25 and 29, instead of the usual average of about 15, but after this date baptisms always exceeded burials, the population rose, and by 1801 there were 880 in the parish, perhaps 600 in the village. In the same time the population of Emsworth had increased to 1,171.

When James Dallaway wrote his local history in 1815 he described Bosham in the following terms:

> The village of Bosham lies at the north-western extremity of the parish, and close upon the creek; the inhabitants are chiefly employed in navigation and fishing.

What Dallaway omitted to say was that the real wealth of the parish came not from the fishery but from agriculture. In 1817, according to Walter Butler at Havant, there were 25 fishing vessels at Bosham, five fewer than at Emsworth, but much greater than the 10 at West Wittering and 16 elsewhere in the harbour. Yet we know little about these fishermen, their boats, relationships and wealth. Only two probate records for Bosham fishermen survive. Edward Boyse, who died in 1720, left goods worth £29 12s. to his widow Elizabeth. His boat must have been small: 'one boat & horse & drag & net & one Ele Spere' worth £1 10s. would indicate an inshore fisherman, possibly using his horse to tow his net through the water as they still do in Frisia today. He did have some wealth, money worth £20, household furniture worth £7, giving a little comfort. John Levitt died in December 1714, leaving £38 19s.: included were a 'boat & nets and fishing boots' worth £6. He owned three guns, so he was probably also a wildfowler; his fishing may only have been part-time as he kept pigs and sheep. The name of one other fisherman is known, as later, Richard Wilkinson, maltster of Bosham, left £10 to Ann, the wife of John Levitt, fisherman, presumably the son of the earlier John Levitt. The mention of a maltster at Bosham in 1734 is an indication that the village did have a part in the export trade in malt at this time, although a century later there was little trade out of Bosham.

Examination of the probate records of the yeomen and husbandmen of Bosham shows exactly where the real wealth of the community lay. When William Silverlock died in 1740 his goods and chattels were worth £980 10s.; almost all was due to the produce of his lands. These were large for the time for he had no less than 92 acres of wheat 'in tillage' worth £78 4s., and two wheat ricks with 17 loads of wheat worth £132. Silverlock was probably the most important farmer on the manor in the mid-18th century, often serving as an official for the Berkeley lords. George Smith who lived at Old Fishbourne was another wealthy man. Dying in 1759, he left some £1,546 to his widow Elizabeth: some £900 of this was 'in bonds'; Elizabeth herself had been wealthy, owning property in Chichester which had come to her husband on their marriage; George was careful to return it to her in this will. These records are further proof of the great prosperity of those who farmed the land around the harbour in the 18th century, and exported their produce to the London market.

In 1815 Dallaway also recorded that Bosham had been granted the right to hold a market on a Thursday under a charter granted by Henry III. He failed to say if the market was still being held then, but it was very likely in abeyance as markets were giving way to permanent shops. By 1845 a number of these had appeared in Bosham; the inhabitants were no longer forced to go to Chichester for their little luxuries.

Although those who farmed the land prospered, the labourers, as elsewhere, did not. In November 1830 when the Swing Riots broke out all along the south coast, Bosham did not escape. The enemy of the labourers was technological change: the new threshing machines would put men out of work, so they had to be destroyed. The Bosham leader was an out-of-work butcher called Edward Goble. Mr Bennett's machine, said to be worth £20, was duly smashed, and the rioters moved on to break more at Chidham and Funtington before the disturbance was ended by the exertions of the Duke of Richmond. Ten Sussex men were later tried and transported; the riots were over.

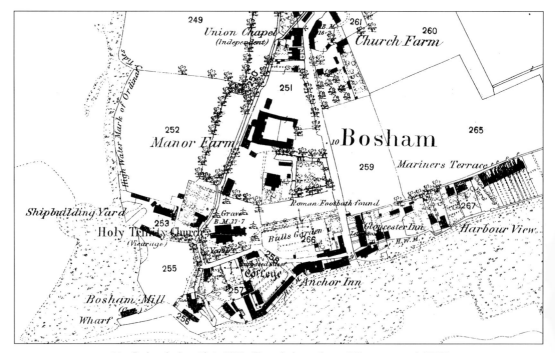

46   *Bosham harbourside in 1875. (From Ordnance Survey 25" map, surveyed 1875.)*

In the 1830s the last of the commons and open fields in the parish were enclosed. This was obviously in the best interests of the farmers, although not always of their men, for this is the period of 'High Farming' when the rising population was fed from Britain's own resources and agriculture flourished, until in 1875 came the influx of cheap American grain. The town labourer obtained cheaper food and the countryside went to ruin.

By 1841 the population of the parish had risen to over 1,000; of these 783 lived in the village, the rest were scattered through the other tithings, from nine at Broadbridge to 90 at Old Fishbourne. Listed in that return are the various branches of the Apps family, boatbuilders

---

BOSHAM is a village and parish, 3 miles west from Chichester, in the hundred of the same name, Western division of the county, rape and county court district of Chichester, Westbourne union, and rural deanery of Boxgrove (third division), diocese and archdeaconry of Chichester. Two branches of the great estuary, Chichester Harbour and Bosham Creek, form the boundaries of the parish on the east, west and south. The London, Brighton and South Coast railway passes through the northern portion of the parish and has a station at Broadbridge, called the Bosham station. The church of the Holy Trinity is chiefly in the Early English style with but little admixture, and consists of chancel, nave of four bays, aisles and a western tower with spire containing 6 bells; in the north wall is a niche, with crocketed ornaments, enclosing a female recumbent figure, of a style not later than the reign of Edward I.; a daughter of Cnut is said to have been buried here, and a woodcut of the coffin and remains, as discovered, is given in Elwes and Robinson's 'Western Sussex': the stalls of the prebendaries form one of the many objects of interest in this ancient church, which was constituted by Henry II. a royal peculiar : there are sittings for 400 persons. The register dates from the year 1557. The living is a vicarage, net yearly value £300, with residence, with 10 acres of glebe, in the gift of the Dean and Chapter of Chichester, and held, since 1845, by the Rev. Henry Mitchell M.A. of Lincoln College, Oxford, F.S.A. rural dean of Boxgrove third division, and surrogate. An establishment of Benedictine canons was founded here and was in existence at the time of the Domesday survey; their possessions, given by Henry I. to William Warlewaste, Bishop of Exeter, were resettled by him on a new basis, and the church enlarged ; the Bishop of Exeter continued to be collated as prebendary of this church, irrespective of the concurrence of the Diocesan, until the dissolution of religious houses. The charities amount to about £28 10s. yearly, viz., Elizabeth Nash's, averaging £16 yearly,

for sick, aged and most needy poor ; Elizabeth Beazley's, of £1 yearly : Day's, of £5 13s. 4d. yearly, both distributed in money ; and Parker's of £4, for educational purposes. Here are the extensive brick, tile and fancy pottery works of A. Cheesman esq. under the management of Robert Hounsom. The pumping station of the Chichester Waterworks Company is situated at Old Fishbourne. Old Park is the property of the Hon. C. P. Fitzhardinge Berkeley. The principal landowners are the Hon C. P. F. Berkeley, who is lord of the manor, Major James Webber Smith, Alfred Cheesman esq. J. J. Johnson esq., Q.C. Mrs. Farndell, J. Godman esq. Mrs. F. Smith, John Heaver esq. and John Baring esq. The soil is rich loam; subsoil, marl. The chief crops are wheat, barley and oats. The area is 3,194 acres of land and 645 water ; rateable value, £8,060 ; the population in 1881 was 1,245.

BROADBRIDGE, 1 mile north west, CREED, east ½ mile, OLD FISHBOURNE, 1 mile east, GOSPORT and WALTON, 1 mile north-east, are tithings belonging to this parish.

Parish Clerk, John Humphrey.

POST OFFICE, Railway station.—George Turner, sub-postmaster. Letters through Chichester, which is the nearest money order and telegraph office; letters arrive at 7.30 a.m. ; dispatched at 12.9 noon & 6.53 p.m. on week days & at 6.53 p.m. on sunday only

WALL LETTER BOX, cleared at 6 p.m. week-days & 11.15 a.m. on sundays

Coroner for the Hundred of Bosham (*comprising the Parishes of Bosham, Chidham, Funtington, West Stoke, Thorney Island & Pilsey Isle*), Alfred Cheesman

National School, Bosham, John Demment, master

National School, Old Fishbourne, Miss Emily Fawcett, mistress

Railway Station, Broadbridge, George Turner, clerk

Carrier, Jacobs, to Chichester daily

PRIVATE RESIDENTS.

Allam Mrs. Old Fishbourne
Arnell John
Baker Richard, Gosport
Burge Mrs
Cheesman Alfred [coroner for the Hundred of Bosham], The Rectory house
Lane Mrs. North villa, Old Fishbourne
Mitchell Rev. Henry M.A., F.S.A. [vicar, rural dean & surrogate], Vicarage
Richardson James
Williams George

COMMERCIAL.

Aldous Harry, grocer
Apps George, shipwright, Gosport
Apps Thomas, ship builder
Aylmore Porter, master mariner
Batchelor Edward, blacksmith
Bloomfield Philip, master mariner
BRICK, TILE, DRAIN PIPE & POTTERY WORKS (Alfred Cheesman, proprietor ; Robert Hounsom, manager)
Brown John, miller (water)
Charles Henry, coal dealer
Collins Edward, *Gloster inn*
Collins Henry, master mariner
Cox Walter William, grocer
Ewen George, bricklayer
Farndell Catherine (Mrs.), farmer

Gatehouse Thomas, miller (steam & water), Broadbridge mill
Gilbey Geoffrey, master mariner
Hallett Tom, grocer & baker, Old Fishbourne
Heather Charles, beer retailer, Walton
Heaver John, farmer, Broadbridge farm
Hounsom Robert, manager to A. Cheesman, Pottery works
Humphrey John, shoe maker
Jacobs John William, assistant overseer
Jarrad John, oyster merchant
Jenkins Thomas, farm bailiff to the Hon. C. P. F. Berkeley, Lower Hone farm
Kearvell Edward, wheelwright & crpntr
Kearvell Stephen, wheelwright & crpntr
Layzell Edward, *Anchor*
March Henry, bricklayer
Marshall William, *Black Boy*, Old Fishbourne
Martin George, master mariner
Martin Robert, beer retailer & shopkeeper & quay master
Newman John, market gardener
Nutter Luke, master mariner, Gosport
Peachey Richard, farmer, Park farm
Perver George, baker
Pudney Charles, master mariner

Redman George, blacksmith
Redman Albt. blacksmith, Old Fishbrne
Reynolds George, shoe maker
Richardson Edward, coal dealer
Richardson Henry, shopkeeper
Rodgers Daniel, thatcher
Singer George, farm bailiff to John Baring esq. Polthooks
Smart Thomas, ship owner
Smith William, master mariner
Stanbrook Thomas, beer retailer, Old Fishbourne
Tillett Jessie, master mariner
Towes Edward, master mariner
Towsend James, *Berkeley Arms*
Trevett Elizabeth (Mrs.), coal merchant & farmer
Trim Chas. *White Swan*, Broadbridge
Walker William, farmer, Colner farm
Wallace William, fishmonger
Welch George, market gardener, Walton
Webb Allan Edmundson, farmer, Church farm
Wells John Clayton, farmer, Hoe farm
Wells Henry, farmer, Leese farm
Williams George, artist
Wingham George, grocer, baker &c. Old Fishbourne
Wood George, smack owner

---

47   Bosham in 1882. (From Kelly's Directory of Sussex, 1882.)

Trade at the Raptackle, Bosham.
48 *Horse-drawn carts loading up from sailing barges in the 1920s. The carts belonged to haulage contractor A.H. Edwards who traded in sand, gravel, coal, coke and wood.*
49 *Small steamers such as this coaster were some of the last major commercial boats to use Chichester Harbour.*

and grocers of Bosham, but even so, in *Kelly's Directory* for 1845, William Apps is still only listed as being a grocer and draper. Not until the end of the decade is his boat-or ship-building trade mentioned, but the full story of William and Thomas Apps will follow later. Another important family mentioned in the 1845 directory was that of Trevett, where John (senior) was a ship-owner, Edward a coasting captain and John (junior) a maltster and grocer. Most of the other tradesmen mentioned were farmers, blacksmiths, inn-keepers or millers.

Despite the fact that there were ship and boatyards at Bosham in the latter part of the 19th century, and the local directories indicate the presence of a small number of coasting skippers, trade from the Raptackle seems to have been very slight in the years before the railway came, and was probably even less thereafter. John Farrant found that in 1836, a year in which Emsworth handled 171 inward coastal cargoes and 140 outward-bound, Bosham saw only four inward-bound cargoes and 19 outward-bound. There would appear to be a number of obvious reasons for this relative decline of the older community. One may be that the charter granted by James II to Chichester, defining the boundaries of the Port and making Dell Quay the only place of lading for foreign cargoes, took trade from Bosham whilst increasing that at Emsworth, which was both within Chichester Harbour but outside the Port. At both Bosham and Dell Quay dues had to be paid, at the former to the manor, at the latter to the corporation. At Emsworth the quays were owned by the local merchants and no such dues were asked for.

Land communications around the harbour had improved by the end of the 18th century. In 1762 came the Cosham-Chichester turnpike, which benefited Emsworth as it passed through the parish; whilst in 1779 the turnpike road from Chichester to Dell Quay was completed. In the 1840s came the London, Brighton and South Coast Railway which took trade from coastal shipping; Bosham's station at Broadbridge was further from the waterfront than those at Emsworth and Chichester, with the latter hard by the Canal Basin.

50   Young Edwardians on Bosham Quay in about 1909.

By 1901 there were 1,149 people in Bosham parish, but living standards of health and sanitation were still medieval in their simplicity. Piped water only came in 1910, a proper sewerage system later. Up to 1914 the fishing industry and the oyster trade remained profitable apart from the hiatus of 1902 caused by the Emsworth oyster scare. The building of small boats continued, but no more coasters were launched. Oyster dredging was a winter trade and, as at Emsworth, many of the fishermen would spend the summer crewing the great yachts at Cowes. More and more the activities of Bosham residents turned towards the support of leisure pursuits. When the building of fishing vessels and wooden sailing coasters ceased, and fishing became less profitable, the boatyards turned to small yachts and dinghies. Today the oyster trade of the whole harbour has almost vanished. Agriculture and horticulture are still practised in the parish and are profitable, but today the greater part of the inhabitants of Bosham form a part of the Chichester dormitory, or else they are involved in leisure activities chiefly concerned with the water. No gallant ship now leaves the Raptackle for London with its cargo of grain or flour ground at the Quay Mill, or sails into port with some sixty tons of coal for which its crew of three men and a boy have risked their lives on a winter voyage from Sunderland.

51   Relic of harbour trade, Bosham. This raised walkway—the Trippit—(photographed in 1995) is said to be built out of stones from all over England and Europe that came into Bosham as ships' ballast.

The Eastern Shore –
New Fishbourne to West Wittering

There were five parishes of varying sizes along the eastern shore of the harbour and, unlike Emsworth or Bosham villages which were always maritime settlements, these parishes were basically agricultural in outlook. It was only after the mid-17th century and the development of the export trade in grain that the harbour became so important to them. Significantly none of these five parishes had its church actually on the waterside. In the cases of Birdham, Itchenor and West Wittering, the village nucleus was a spring feeding a stream which flowed into an inlet from the harbour; this situation also applied at Warblington. At Fishbourne, the sites of both the old and the new settlements were determined by the presence of copious springs which still feed into the head of Fishbourne Creek. No village is associated with Apuldram church, and there may never have been a nuclear settlement in the parish; here the scattered homesteads would draw their water from shallow wells dug into the gravel subsoil. The soil in all the parishes was, and is, immensely fertile. When subsistence agriculture was replaced by farming for the market, the inhabitants of this district became adept at growing far more grain than they could consume and then exporting it to London. The harbour was convenient for this trade and fortunes could be, and were, regularly made.

The parish of New Fishbourne was a comparatively late creation, only gaining its church in the 13th century. The name comes from the fish found in the streams which flow into the harbour at this point. Originally the site of the Roman port of Chichester, the settlement had been split just before the Conquest, when Harold's brother Tostig was granted land there, whilst Old Fishbourne stayed in the manor of Bosham. By 1086 Tostig's land had been granted to the French abbey of Séez. In the 15th century the lands of all foreign abbeys were sequestrated and the descent after 1415 is complicated, but by 1684 the lordship had come into the possession of Sir Thomas Miller whose family had risen to wealth and position as clothiers and then maltsters. The ownership of New Fishbourne would give them a place in the country, and also—despite the grant to Chichester of a charter giving their wharf at Dell Quay the right to be the only 'place of lading' in the Port of Chichester—a place where barges could call.

The population of the parish of only 597 acres was small until the growth of Chichester itself merged with both Fishbournes. In 1086 there were just 17 villein families, perhaps some 70 souls. There was slow growth throughout the Middle Ages; in the mid-13th century some 22 named persons paid tithe, giving an estimated population of about one hundred. The rental of 1460 shows 25 households or about 120 persons yet, by the time of the Compton census of 1676, numbers had fallen to about 50 in the parish. This is probably too low. Unfortunately the

Hearth Tax records for the parish are indecipherable. Then by 1811, as Chichester's own population increased, New Fishbourne had a population of 252 which had grown to 366 by 1901. Thereafter statistics show less the growth of Fishbourne, more the growth of Chichester.

In the late 18th and early 19th centuries the agriculture of the parish flourished, as did its mills, of which more anon. From at least 1800 another trade had developed. In the north of the parish along Clay Lane lie beds of Reading Clay. By the end of the 18th century this clay was being fully exploited, and coal was imported at the small wharf alongside the mill for brick-making. In 1833 William Goodleve announced that he had taken over the business from Onslow Wakeford, who had been running it for some 30 years. He offered to sell coal from his barges at 28s. per chaldron (roughly a ton). He also exported bricks to other points in the harbour. The trade to Fishbourne Mill seems to have continued in a small way until the 1920s. Going to the foot of Mill Lane today and seeing the creek full of reeds, it does not seem possible that only 70 years ago this was a working quay where coal and grain were landed and flour and bricks were taken away.

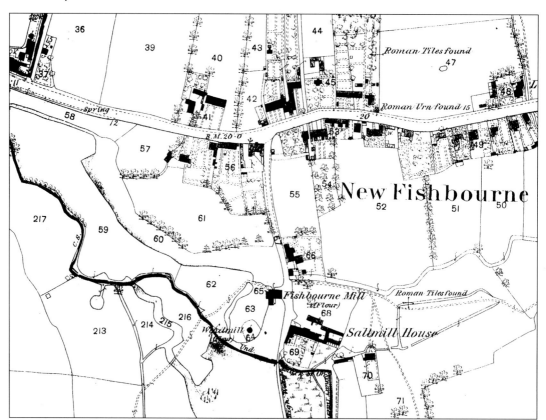

52   Fishbourne Creek in 1875. Water traffic used the quay by the watermill until the 1920s.
(From Ordnance Survey 25" map, surveyed 1875.)

Apuldram—sometimes spelt Appledram—is 'the place of apple trees', so in Saxon times there must have been orchards hereabouts. The parish originally contained 937 acres, its northern boundary being the river Lavant, its southern the brook which flowed into the Salterns. In the north the soil is very fertile brickearth over chalk, but south of Dell Quay the subsoil changes to Reading Clay. On the Bosham side of the harbour is the last original woodland, Old

Park Wood; it seems likely that this side, too, remained wooded until perhaps the 17th century. The clay outcrop continues towards Copperas Point. Copperas is iron sulphate and found in thin seams in the clay; this was dug out and left to weather and the copperas crystals collected, to be used as a mordant in the late medieval dyeing industry. When Dallaway wrote about Apuldram in 1815 he described the land as 'rich ... excepting towards the south, where it is marshy'. It was on this marshy area that the Apuldram salterns were situated.

Apuldram was one of the prebends of Bosham; the prebendary filled the role of rector, drawing the tithes and appointing a vicar to take the services. In 1291 the value of this prebend was £20 per year. The church was built in the 13th century as a chapel of ease within the parish of Bosham; not until 1447 did it have its own graveyard. When the college at Bosham was abolished after the Reformation the then vicar stayed on as curate of Apuldram, although it was not until the late 18th century that the bishop recognised the office and officially appointed the incumbent of Apuldram to a perpetual curacy.

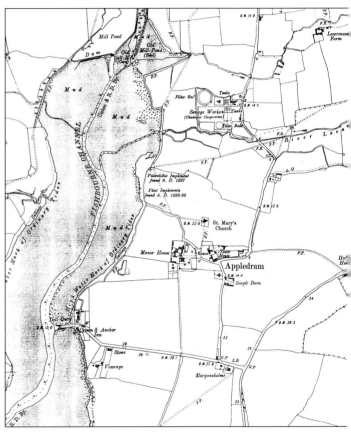

Father Richard Ratcliff, who wrote a short history of the parish, estimated its population as 220 in 1321 but only 150 in 1432; such a fall suggests that the Black Death had struck hard here, or that the land had been turned over from corn to sheep for the benefit of the Chichester woollen industry. The population had declined to about 60 in 1678, whilst in 1724 the curate claimed that there were only eight families in the parish. This would mean that only some 50 persons lived there, but the first census of 1801 showed 136; it was still only 134 in 1901, having reached a peak of 188 in 1831.

A small population in a large acreage usually meant wealth for the few, so it should be no surprise that in 1748 the yeoman Thomas Chatfield of Crouch End Farm had goods and chattels worth several hundred pounds. He rented the land for £205 per year, although at the time of his death this remained unpaid. His son and heir was also called Thomas Chatfield. He had been left some property before his father's death and stated that the whole inventory should really amount to some £500. His household goods were valued at £100, there was stock worth £200, £90 in cash, £80 in money owing, and the grain in the rick, the barn and the ground were worth another £200.

53 Appledram—otherwise Apuldram—in 1906. Within the parish is Dell Quay, for centuries the official landing place in the Port of Chichester. (From Ordnance Survey 6" map, surveyed 1906.)

In the Middle Ages the manor of Apuldram had belonged to the Ryman family—hence the name of Rymans for their house—but by the early 19th century, whilst the landowner was the important London politician William Hamilton, it was the Freeland family who leased the land and who were the dominant element in the parish.

In 1680, when the royal charter defining the bounds of the Port of Chichester was issued, the wharf at Dell Quay was described as being 90 feet long by 49 feet broad, not a very large facility for the chief landing place in the harbour. In time warehouses were built for the storage of grain, the first in 1698. By the mid-18th century there were three, one to the north and two to the south. Chichester Corporation, hoping to make money, charged dues on goods landed, citizens paying less than 'foreigners'. In contrast, as Longcroft pointed out in the 1850s, no dues were charged at Emsworth, where by the mid-18th century the facilities were improved. In 1757 the corporation decided to add a crane, but it was never very successful and had disappeared by the end of the century, by which time there was a windmill on the quay. Communications with Chichester were much improved when the turnpike road from Midhurst was extended south of the city to Dell Quay in 1779. When Horsfield wrote in 1835, he said that Dell Quay was 'of less importance since the establishment of the Arundel and Portsmouth canal'. This was a point that had worried the corporation, so that they insisted on being paid a proportion of the tolls collected at the Canal Basin. Dell Quay still received a few cargoes brought by barge right up to the start of the last war. The last steamers piloted by George Haines of Itchenor ceased to call in the late 1920s. Today Dell Quay is the property of the Chichester Harbour Conservancy.

Birdham, anciently Bridham, takes it name from the presence of birds. At 1,811 acres the parish was of medium size, the soil, brickearth over London Clay, very productive. In 1086 there were only 13 families, so the population was small. There was a mill there; exactly where

54   Dell Quay in the late 1920s. Loading grain on to one of the last coastal steamers to use the harbour.

it was no one knows, but it had disappeared by the end of the Middle Ages. Although the probate records for the parish show that a miller lived there in 1687, Nicholas Read was actually a yeoman farmer who had the lease of a windmill at Up Marden, or so his will says, and it is unlikely that the men of Birdham took their grain there to be ground; they probably went to Bosham.

By the mid-17th century the population was some 140-50; by 1801 this had risen to 361; later in the mid-19th century it was to reach the 530s, but by 1901 it had dropped to below 400, a pattern which is typical of purely rural parishes during the 19th century. Two developments occurred to enhance 18th-century prosperity: the building of the tide mill at what is now Birdham Pool in about 1767, and the enclosure of Birdham Common under the auspices of the bishop of Chichester, who had the principal interest in the matter in 1791. The Common started at roughly what is now the northern end of the Birdham straight, and ended just north of the turning to Itchenor. Wherever there is a particularly straight line of road, if the Romans did not build it, then enclosure commissioners probably laid it out.

The church of St James is situated next to the village green where a pump used to stand. A spring, now covered, is at the northern corner of the green. Originally this spring water formed the headwaters of the stream which flowed down to Birdham Pool. The church dates from the 14th century, but there was an earlier building on the site. To the south of Birdham there used to be a small parish called East Itchenor; in 1086 there were three families there. By 1291 both East Itchenor and Birdham had churches; indeed the former was the richer of the

55 *By Birdham Mill in about 1905.*

two, worth £8 to Birdham's £5 6s. 8d. However, by 1441, East Itchenor's population had declined to such an extent that the bishop of Chichester combined the two parishes. East Itchenor church became a chapel within Birdham parish, but by 1640 it had been demolished. Today nothing remains and the site is lost.

From the late 17th century to the late 19th century when the agricultural slump began, the yeomen of Birdham, too, were extremely wealthy. In 1710, for example, Richard Fivens had goods and chattels worth £999 12s. He was running a farm of considerable size, far from being a peasant holding. He had 100 acres under wheat, 32 acres of peas, 40 acres of oats and eight acres of tares. There was no barley in the ground as it was April and presumably had not yet been sown, so he must have had at least 180 acres under crops at a time when a normal holding elsewhere might be 30 acres or less. He also ran 250 sheep and lambs, 26 cattle and seven calves, 20 hogs, and owned five horses and four mares with appropriate harnesses for carts and ploughs. When Daniel Richards died in 1730 his goods were worth over £1,600, of which £1,131 was 'due to the deceased on Mortgages Bonds and other Similar Interests', showing that the wealth he had gained from agriculture had been invested in other enterprises. His son, Richard Richards, died only four years later. His goods only amounted to £665 because the amount of money on 'Bonds and Mortgages' had dropped to a mere £475 as a result of the legacies of his father.

The population of the parish scarcely increased between 1901 and the end of the Second World War; Birdham remained rural although the first intimation of what was to come was the creation of the marina at Birdham Pool in 1937. Today, whilst agriculture and horticulture remain important, many of the local inhabitants are involved in leisure pursuits associated with the harbour.

Itchenor takes its name from the Saxon chieftain Icca who first resettled the district after the collapse of Roman Britain. The parish is still officially West Itchenor, despite the fact that the vill of East Itchenor disappeared in the 15th century. Before the Norman Conquest the manor of West Itchenor was a part of the greater manor of Bosham. By 1086 there were just six families, or some 30 persons, presumably living around the spring to the south of the church. The lord was Roger Montgomery, but he had let the estate to his man Warin. Later West Itchenor came into the ownership of the Rymans of Apuldram, but by the 17th century the manorial rights seem to have lapsed.

In about 1175 the then lord of West Itchenor, Hugh d'Esturmy, persuaded the bishop of Chichester and the prebendary of Westringes (or Witterings) to allow him to build a chapel on the manor. By the end of the century this had developed into a proper parish church dedicated to St Nicholas, the patron saint of seamen, and with its own graveyard. The parish was small, only 546 acres. There may never have been a single village, but three small settlements: one by the church, one at Shipton Green and—a later development—one by the shore at the end of The Street. In the mid-17th century the population seems to have been between 50 and 60. Already there was a shipwright at the edge of the channel, and, although in the 18th century there was a considerable amount of ship-building, only 161 persons lived in the parish in 1801. This grew to some 250 in the mid-19th century, then declined to about 120 in 1901. After the end of the Napoleonic wars there are no further records of large ships being built at Itchenor. Although the church records show that James Apps, of the Apps family, described variously as 'ship-builder' or 'boat-builder', lived there in the 1820s, he may actually have worked at the Bosham yard. In the 1851 census there is also a mention of a boat-builder at Itchenor, 'employing one man and two apprentices', but he does not appear in earlier or later returns. Permanent boat-building and repair seems to have restarted with Haines' yard in about 1912.

56 Itchenor House. The Duke of Richmond's 18th-century yacht-ing lodge. This photograph was taken in the 1870s.

57 (inset) Expenses for the sloop Goodwood *in 1788. Oper-ated by the Duke of Richmond's estate, the sloop's home base was at Itchenor.*

In the late 18th century the 3rd Duke of Richmond bought land in West Itchenor and built Itchenor House as his yachting lodge; he also built a salt-water bath on the shore near where the Conservancy Office now stands. In the Goodwood Papers in the West Sussex Record Office are the master's accounts of the Duke's sloop, the *Goodwood*, for the years 1783-1793, during which time the house was built and Goodwood House was being enlarged. She seems to have spent a considerable amount of time bringing stone from various places for both build-ing works. Thus in 1787 she brought 144 tons of stone from Swanage; other voyages saw her carrying granite from Guernsey and stone and bricks from Plymouth. Her crew seems to have consisted of a master, a mate and four hands. This fact, and the stone cargo from Swanage, whose weight is listed, would suggest a vessel of some 150 tons, typical of the larger craft then using the harbour.

When the Duke died, officially childless, he left Itchenor House and Park to Henrietta Anne Leclerc, whom he named as his natural daughter. She later married General John Dorrien and lived in some style. When Horsfield wrote about the parish in 1835, Mrs. Dorrien, by now a widow, still lived at Itchenor House, but Horsfield had little to say

George Haines of Itchenor

Now to introduce you to the man who can tell you most about Itchenor. Turn left after leaving the village and you will come to a long wooden jetty which takes you to the ferry and thence over the water to Bosham.

Seventy-six years old George Haines, harbour-master, ferryman, and scores of other official posts, was just tying up his ferry boat—a small rowing boat—on to the side of the jetty. Nearby, was the Tinamu, the biggest yacht in the harbour, and it seemed to dwarf the ferry boat into insignificance.

Somehow, George does not look like a seafaring man, despite the fact that he spent 16 years roughing the oceans. Rather small in stature and slightly thin, he has a handsome bearded face. He was wearing the traditional seaman's clothes.

'Things have changed,' he told me. 'I was born at Portsmouth and spent 16 years at sea and I have been in Itchenor for 45 years. It is only during the last few years that all these yachts have come into the harbour. When I was a boy there were only a few coal boats.'

I asked George to tell me some stories about his sea life, but he would say nothing more than that he was once shipwrecked after a fierce gale which lasted four days without ceasing.

George lives in a quaint little cottage near the ferry and he told me that this was once Itchenor's inn. Indeed, one could imagine the carefree sailors entering that little place when it had a thatched roof that nearly touched the ground. Next door is the old customs house and this receives a thorough washing during winter gales when the sea lashes up against its walls.

58   *George Haines of Itchenor in about 1940. George was a man of many parts in the harbour earlier this century. As the Itchenor pilot he took commercial sailing craft and steamers up the shallow channel from Itchenor to Dell Quay. His grandson, George, who took over the Haines' family boat-building business with his brother Kenneth, remembers as a boy how frightened he felt bumping over the harbour bottom on one of his grandfather's last steamer trips to Dell Quay in about 1930.*

George's house is named 'Ferryside' and above the entrance is a door. 'This often puzzles people,' said George, with a chuckle, 'but we use it for storing all sorts of things to do with the boats.'

George likes to look back on the days when he was a seaman. 'It was a hard life' he said, 'but it was a good one. Things are all quickness to-day. Yes, and in ten years time men won't know how to splice a wire.'

Southern Weekly News, 4 July 1936

about West Itchenor: 'the village, which contains nothing of interest, is situated six miles and a half S.W. by W. of Chichester. No public road runs through it.'

The wealth of most of the other parishes lay in the soil, but the richest persons in West Itchenor in the 18th century tended to be 'mariners', which probably means 'merchants trading by sea'; thus John Woodland who died in 1699 left goods worth £435 which included 'the half part of the *Expedition* snow' (a small two-masted vessel not unlike a brig) worth £40. He had recently sold shares in two other craft for £50. Such an inventory suggests that not all the trade in the Port of Chichester was confined to Dell Quay.

The story of Itchenor would not be complete without mention of the families of Rogers, Haines and Darley. The former had run the ferry to Bosham since the early 19th century and lived in 'Ferryside', which is now the Conservancy Office. In the 1880s George Haines, born at West Wittering, and later a seaman employed in the Newcastle coal trade, married Rebecca Rogers. The couple took over the ferry, the Haines family running it until it closed in the 1950s. (It was opened again by the Conservancy in 1976.) It was this George Haines who was to act as virtual harbourmaster, pilot and collector of tolls until Chichester Corporation took over the running of the harbour in the 1930s. The name of Darley, according to local legend, first appears in the reign of Charles II when the royal yacht *Fubbs* is said to have been based at Itchenor but, as will be argued later, the story is probably mere legend. The first Darley reference in the Itchenor parish registers appears in 1755 when Jane, the daughter of John and Ann Darley, was baptised on 3 August. In the early 19th cen-tury the Darleys are said to have been 'mari-ners'; later they were merchants in coal and grain. Until recently they ran the chandlery and owned much land to the east of The Street.

Itchenor has been the site of a Customs House for some considerable time; today one is there, but infrequently manned. Many of the inhabitants of modern Itchenor are involved in the recreational activities of the harbour, having moved to the village to take part in maritime pursuits.

West Wittering was one of the earlier Saxon settlements in the harbour area. There was apparently a church there as early as AD 740; the name comes from Wihthere, and both East and West Wittering in early times were called 'Wihthringes'. It was one of the original manors given to the cathedral at Selsey, and remained the property of the bishops of Chi-chester until 1522 when they leased the manor and their house at Cakeham to the Ernley fam-ily. The parish contains 2,286 acres. At the time of Domesday there was a mill on the manor, probably situated somewhere on the brook which leads from the spring, near the small patch of village green. Today no water mill, or trace of one, remains, although in Budgen's

59 *Cakeham Tower, West Wittering. Built in the early 16th century, this Tudor landmark close to the harbour entrance is still used as a navigation point by seamen today.*

map of 1724 a windmill is marked south of the village. The Domesday population was perhaps 150, but could be less, depending on whether lands held by the bishop's men are within or without the modern parish. In the mid-17th century an estimate would put the population at about 200, a figure which had doubled by 1801, increased to 655 by 1881, and, with the decline of English agriculture, fallen to 494 by 1901. More recently, in line with present trends, the population has risen comfortably, West Wittering being a part of the Chichester dormitory area, but, as in the case of Birdham and Itchenor, this is a post-war development; from 1901 to 1945 the area was a part of the rural backwater of south-west Sussex.

End to Harbour?

The West Wittering Harbour Reclamation Scheme is to come before Parliament in the form of a private bill ...

Briefly the scheme falls into three main divisions. The water which floods the flats at high tide is to be shut out by a timber barrier. The rife is to be deepened and converted into a canal with locks and mooring basins. The level of the flats is to be raised and converted into a golf course, with a hotel and clubhouse close to the point of the West Wittering Spit - the original Spit Head, a name now applied only to the water between the head and the Isle of Wight.

The practical objections to a sea-wall are evident to one who, like myself, has lived in West Wittering for twenty years. I have seen the coast line change in that time ...

An examination of documents in the Record Office shows how the channels and sandbanks have altered during the centuries at the point with which the scheme proposes to deal. One small instance will show that West Wittering has some importance as a port in the fourteenth century. Edward II at Newcastle, required certain produce in 1319. The Archbishop of Canterbury 'lent' the king 90 quarters of wheat, 15 of beans and five of peas, which were sent from Nyetimber, Slindon and Tangmere to West Wittering, where they were loaded on to a ship belonging to William Bateman of Dunwich. Old residents here can remember coal brought and landed at Snow Hill where, even at high tide, nothing larger than a dinghy could land to-day.

Schemes have been started before and found impracticable because of our ever-changing shore. Last century, there was a scheme for building a channel port at West Wittering, to run a service between that place and Cherbourg. It came to nothing.

Once, the sea came up every high tide to the churchyard wall and fishermen tied their boats to iron rings set in the wall. The church is now half a mile inland, but tradition says that boats will be moored there again...

West Wittering desires to keep its harbour because, as Mr. Hugh Fausset wrote in *The Times*, the natural beauty of the harbour is the very life-blood of West Wittering. The flats over which the water washes twice each day are an ever-changing scene of loveliness, whether they are pink with thrift and sea-stocks, or lavender-hued with statice, or bright green with orache ...

Many of us love this scene with a passionate devotion hard to put into words ... Must we lose it? If so, it will not be without a struggle ...

L.F. Ramsey, *Sussex County Magazine*, vol. 8 (1934)

Because the parish of West Wittering is on the coast there has been some erosion of the coastline and, in common with Hayling and Thorney Islands, the Inquest of the Ninth of 1340 claimed that the church had lost value since 1292 by reason of 'land lost to the sea'. The parishioners were more specific: land worth seven marks had been 'absorbed by the sea'; land worth five marks had been 'wasted by sand', and as an extra and a dig at their lord the bishop, 'land worth 11 marks has been damaged by the conies from the Bishop's Warren'. The latter was on Cockbush Common, which has now mostly disappeared, for it lay to the west of what is now East Head, behind the gravel spit washed away between 1900 and 1926. Dallaway, writing in 1815, said that he thought land half a mile to the south of the then shoreline had been lost to the sea, but he did not suggest when this had occurred. Much of what was lost was not in fact of any great agricultural value.

More recently the continuing problem of containing the erosion at East Head has had to be faced. When the National Trust took over this vulnerable spit of land at the harbour entrance in 1966, it had recently been broken through by the sea. The Trust, with the great assistance of volunteer workers under the leadership of Sidney Searle, undertook major reclamation

60   Opening of the boardwalk at East Head in November 1992. A joint enterprise between Chichester Harbour Conservancy and the National Trust. Shown here are Connie Scott, representing the Trust, and Lieutenant-Commander Richard Wilson, Chairman of the Conservancy.

work to build up the land. Today the Conservancy works closely with the Trust to ensure constant vigilance, and the position seems to have been stabilised. But in case of a future emergency, contigency funds are available through an appeal launched by harbour yachtsmen and the Solent Protection Society.

Land to the north of a line from Snow Hill Creek to Cakeham is brickearth on London Clay; to the south are the sands and gravels of the Bracklesham Beds, suitable for rough grazing, but before the present century generally not considered worth cultivation.

Again, as is the case of Birdham, the real wealth of the parish from the 17th to the late 19th centuries came from agriculture; there were a few fishermen at Snow Hill, one will be mentioned later, and Butler in 1817 reported that there were some ten fishing boats owned in the parish, but the probate inventories tell a tale of yeomen possessing considerable wealth. The richest of all was Richard Guy who died in 1738, worth, so it was claimed, over £1,600 (although addition of the various figures shows it to be nearer £1,480). His farm, like that of Richard Fivens, was large for the time: 125 acres of sown crops, half being wheat—'60 acres of wheat growing' valued at £120—and he also had five horses to work the farm and a quantity of cattle, sheep and pigs. The value of his farm stock was over £400, of his household goods £220, and, like Fivens, he had money on loan, in this case over £860. With a market at London and good communications through the harbour, arable farming could once more be seen to pay, and pay well. Even a farmer such as John Earwicker, who died in 1734 with less than 100 acres, could leave goods worth almost £200, and the Napper family were equally fortunate. When John Napper died in 1755 his goods were worth £821 13s. 3d., and included 'a note of hand for £417', whilst his clothing and 'money in the house' came to £105.

By the early years of the present century West Wittering was still an agricultural parish, although farming was languishing, but it was also becoming 'a nice healthy place to live'. Amongst those who came here for the good of their health was Henry Royce who left Derby in 1912, came to West Wittering in 1917, and remained there until his death in 1933. It was at his house called 'Elmstead' that the famous Rolls Royce 'R' engine was first discussed, so it was appropriate that the turning beacon in the Schneider Trophy contests in the late '20s and early '30s (won by British Seaplanes mounting Rolls-Royce engines) was at West Wittering. By the late 1930s the pattern for the future was set; the first holiday camp sites appeared, and recreation replaced agriculture as the chief source of revenue in the parish.

IX

From Chidham to the Hermitage

Apart from the extreme south of the Chidham peninsula and Thorney Island, where the brickearth topsoil overlies the Reading Clay, the soil along the northern shore of the harbour is brickearth over chalk, part of the extremely fertile Fareham - Selsey Brickearth Plain, considered to be one of the finest light soils in the whole country. In this area lie the three parishes of Chidham, West Thorney and Westbourne with its hamlets of Nutbourne, Prinsted and the Hermitage. The two former are situated on the spring-line, but the latter is on the Sussex side of the Ems opposite Emsworth; Westbourne, whilst not on the harbour, was once at the head of the tidewater on the Ems and as such deserves a mention.

Chidham church and the handful of houses which surround it is in the centre of the peninsula and originally stood at the head of a small inlet from the Bosham Channel, now filled in. There is ground water just below the surface, so wells could easily be dug, and this ground water is the source of the village pond to the east of the settlement. Chidham formed part of the estate of Bosham church and remained the property of the bishop of Exeter until after the dissolution of the college when it was sold. By 1707 it had come into the possession of the Earls of Scarborough, and in the early 19th century was owned by William Padwick whose attempt to embank the upper reaches of the Bosham Channel has already been told. Chidham, being one of the prebends of the college, was served by a vicar appointed by the prebendary until the dissolution, after which the existing vicar stayed in office and the succession continued normally.

As the Domesday Book entry is for the whole estate of Bosham church it is difficult to assess the size of the population at that date for what was to become the parish of Chidham; at a rough guess it might be around 100, which is quite populous for the time. In 1676 the Compton census indicates that some 130 persons lived in the parish which then comprised some 1,525 acres. By 1801 this had increased to 209, which rose to over 300 by the middle of the century and declined to 260 by 1901. Today the population of the old parish centre is small and most of the inhabitants live along the line of the present A259.

From Saxon times until the present century the chief occupation of the population was agriculture, and farming is still very important. In 1817 Walter Butler recorded that there was a single fishing boat at Chidham. Probate records, census returns and trade directories all confirm both the agricultural interest of the parishioners and the fact that, from the time that the old coast road became important, there was a blacksmith there. In the 17th and 18th centuries most men were yeomen or farmers; by the 19th they were farmers and farm labourers.

In the 17th and 18th centuries the most noted agricultural family was that of Kennett; the first whose name occurs in the records was Robert who died in 1625, leaving goods worth £158. Nothing could indicate better the rise in living standards in the 17th and 18th centuries than the contrast between his inventory and that of Henry Kennett who died in 1742. Robert's

61   *Thorney Island and the mainland in 1778. For its accuracy and topographical detail this map, by Thomas Yeakell and William Gardner, is a landmark in 18th-century surveying. The original is at a scale of 2 inches to 1 mile. The meticulous hydrography for the harbour is based on a manuscript chart made by, or for, Sir Piercy Brett in 1759.*

household goods were worth a bare £30; the rest was made up of the value of his stock and the grain in the fields and barns. His stock comprised 'horse beasts' worth £17, 48 sheep, 12 'kine' and nine hogs. His grain, wheat, barley and vetches were worth £72, his clothes and money £3 Henry Kennett, on the other hand, had goods worth £232; included in his household possessions were '12 large silver spoons' worth £9 2s. Altogether his personal goods were worth some £90 of the total sum. He grew and sold wheat and barley, kept hogs for bacon for the household, owned a few cattle, but no sheep, and apparently made cider as he had '5 syder casks' worth £1 5s. Perhaps the most interesting of all the entries is the complete list of his clothes which included '1 old hat, 2 old pair of breeches, 1 ordinary grey drugget coat, 1 fustian frock, 5 old shirts, 5 old pair of stockings, 2 pair of shoes, 2 pair of boots'; with other items all were valued at £2 2s.

Connected with Chidham, and buried there in 1695, was John Edes, maltster of Chichester, who was responsible for commencing the building of what is today known as Edes House which stands in front of County Hall at Chichester. As he died in September 1695, and the house is said to have been completed in 1696, it would appear that he never saw its completion, let alone lived in it. The Edes family owned Chidmere House in Chidham from 1688 to 1788 and there are memorials to the family in Chidham church. Another 18th-century inhabitant of Chidham was Richard Sone, son of John Sone, of East Leigh Farm in Warblington. He married Mary Midlane at Havant in 1736, the daughter of a long established Havant family. Richard was buried at Chidham in 1748, and his widow died in 1787, aged 87, in occupation of both the Parsonage and Chidmere farms.

Today in Chidham there are horticultural and market gardens on either side of the A259. There are still important farms in the peninsula, and from the point of view of the Conservancy and its remit there is the Cobnor Activities Centre. This, and the wheelchair path alongside the harbour at Cobnor, owe much to the support of the late Martin Beale of Cobnor House, a member of both the Conservancy and the Advisory Committee for many years, and at different times chairman of both.

Thorney Island, the Isle of Thorns, formed the whole of the parish of West Thorney, which, before the enclosure of the Deeps, contained some 1,200 acres. The parish is West Thorney, because near Pagham Harbour there used to be a vill called East Thorney which was

62   Cobnor Activities Centre provides residential sail-training facilities for schools and is specially equipped for teaching the disabled, with wheelchair access on local footpaths. All these facilities were made possible by land made available by Martin Beale of Cobnor House.

63   Martin Beale of Cobnor was a much-loved personality around the harbour which he loved with a passion since a boy. Farmer, countryman, sportsman, and a most intrepid sailor, he brought all his enthusiasms to bear on the Harbour Conservancy as the first Chairman of the consultative Advisory Committee, and later Conservancy Chairman between 1978 and 1981. His gift for encouraging others to share his own love for the harbour bore fruit in his work to set up the Cobnor Activities Centre. Here, proudly displaying the Cobnor emblem, Martin is sailing with his wife, Ann, and Geoffrey Godber, Clerk to the Conservancy.

one of the prebends of Chichester Cathedral, and the church needed to distinguish between the two. In 1086 Thorney Island formed part of the estates of Bosham church which had let it as a manor to a man called Mauger. At that time there were some 32 peasant families, which could indicate that the population was about 150, almost twice as many as lived there in 1676 when the Compton census suggested that there were some 80 persons; this had dropped to 71 by the time of the first census of 1801, which also listed just ten occupied houses. The fall of population during the Middle Ages may have been due in part to the ravages of the Black Death and the subsequent change from arable cultivation to the rearing of sheep to support the local cloth industry. In addition some 40 acres of land were said to have been 'lost to the sea' between 1291 and 1340, when the jurors for the 'taxation of the ninth' gave this as an excuse for the fact that the value of the church's income had fallen between the two dates. On the other hand, medieval men were just as anxious as we are today to explain why our taxes should be lower, so perhaps we ought not to pay too much attention to such claims.

64   *Thorney Island military cemetery.*

The church of St Nicholas stands close to the shore of Thorney Channel. The oldest part of the present building is thought to date from the early 12th century, but there could well have been an earlier church on the site. As Thorney Island was the site of an important RAF station during the last war there is a small military cemetery in a corner of the churchyard where 72 service war casualties were buried, including 21 German aircrew.

Because the lord of the manor died in 1222 without a male heir, the estate was divided amongst his three sisters which had a considerable effect later. Both Dallaway in 1815, and Horsfield in 1835, were insistent that the soil of Thorney Island produced excellent crops of wheat, but pointed out that the fields had only been enclosed in 1811. This late development was most likely due to the difficulty of getting all three of the manorial lords to agree. Butler states that in 1817 there was one fishing vessel owned in Thorney, suggesting that the inhabitants were more interested in the land than the water, yet in 1340 the rector claimed a tithe of fish, the only known local instance. Pilsey Island is recorded at that time as being 'the resort of wild fowl', but in the late 19th century, according to a local report, sheep were pastured there, and the Itchenor ferryman would row across to take the shepherds to check on their flocks.

The 18th-century probate records for West Thorney show much the same pattern as those of the other local parishes; the wealthier men were yeomen or husbandmen. Thus, when he died in December 1709, Thomas Bolton had £28 of 'wheat in the ground', and the rest of his last autumn's crop of wheat, barley, pease and oats still in his barn was worth £44 more. His livestock included four horses with their harness, 11 cattle and eight swine, but no sheep. Out of an inventory worth £152 his household goods were worth less than £20. Twenty years later John Bolton left goods worth £282. His 'wheat in the ground' was worth £63 and, in addition to his 6 horses, 18 cattle and swine he also kept some sheep. His household goods were worth

30 and his 'money and clothes' were valued at £26 10s. more; he seems to have been more prosperous, probably because the grain trade to London was now well established.

Kelly's Directory for 1878 records just one farmer on Thorney, presumably because the enclosures had changed the pattern of landholding. From 71 in 1801 the population had risen to 93 in 1861. The enclosure of the Deeps in the 1870s, whilst increasing the acreage, did little to help increase the population, yet by 1901 this had risen to 148.

In the last quarter of the 19th century a further attempt was made at land reclamation; this time it was the area now known as the Nutbourne Marshes. It failed, but traces of the endeavour remain in the form of Stakes Island where the Conservancy has tried to help the Little Tern to breed, but without much success. For the first 30 years of the present century Thorney remained a quiet agricultural backwater; even the reclamation of the Deeps, which

65   Great Deep, looking eastwards from the Emsworth-Thorney road. Formerly Thorney Island was linked to the mainland by a causeway across Little Deep and Great Deep. A roadway now crosses the Deeps since reclamation work gained land from the harbour.

had enabled a proper road to replace the old Wadeway from the foot of King Street in Emsworth, was not all that helpful as the thoroughfare was owned by the Padwicks, lords of the manor, who kept it private and from time to time locked the gate. Then in 1935 the government decided that Thorney Island was just the place for a new military air base for the inevitable war against Hitler, and by 1937 the RAF was installed and the civilian population started to leave.

The hamlets of Nutbourne and Prinsted in the parish and manor of Westbourne lie on the mainland to the north of Thorney Island. The former is situated on what is now called the Ham Brook, which drains what was Hambrook Common, but the name of the stream must have been changed as the place name 'Nutbourne' means 'the stream amidst the nut trees'. Nutbourne was a sub-manor within the manor of Westbourne; its lord had his own court, but

RAF Thorney Island
66 *(top)   Chichester Harbour's largest building. The imposing officers' mess shortly before its opening in 1938.*
67 *(left)   RAF commemorative window, Thorney Island church.*

had to pay 12d. yearly to the lord of Westbourne to prove that the latter was his overlord. The Domesday reference for Westbourne mentions four mills. One of these was at Nutbourne, presumably on the Ham Brook, and probably just south of the A259 where the stream passes under the road and runs alongside Farm Lane. It would appear to be only towards the end of the 17th century that the later tide mill, of which more hereafter, was constructed.

In the 18th century Nutbourne was a small agricultural community. In the mid-17th century, according to the Sussex Hearth Tax return of 1670, there were 12 households paying the tax and a further 12 who did not. No house had more than three hearths so no one was obviously rich. Such a return would indicate a population of about 120, but later figures are hard to come by as they merge with Westbourne itself. The probate records

Sad Scene

Thorney. Alas, the village has flown away at the bidding of the Flying Age. We found hundreds of men pulling it down to set up a station for the RAF. It was one of the saddest of the sad little scenes we came upon in all our journeyings. Once an island, a little land snatched from the sea has made it a peninsula, and on it 150 people have lived. They looked across the water to Bosham and the spire of Chichester, a pleasing scene with the birds feeding on the mud flats.

They were rung to church by one of the oldest bells still ringing in these islands, and a fine little church they had, standing by the harbour in a forlorn little churchyard. It has the hand of the Saxon and the Norman in its walls, though as we see it it is chiefly 13th century. Happily, it is the one thing the Air Ministry has not pulled down, and the little sanctuary stands alone, as the sign and symbol that even in the Flying Age there are things that were here before men flew and will remain when the last bomb has fallen from the skies.

Arthur Mee, *Sussex* (1937)

Culture Shock

It is now 14 years since the Vietnamese left Thorney Island and those of us who had the privilege of working there during that time often wonder what became of the people who were so much a part of our lives during the two-year contract made via the Home Office on behalf of the nation. The Vietnamese came mainly from Hong Kong camps and few were true Boat People. During that time we resettled nearly 2,000 refugees.

At that time culture shock was unknown to us and perhaps not realised by senior staff. The cold, damp winters were difficult for the refugees. Catapults were discouraged, but the medical centre would, on occasion, send out heart-felt pleas to stop chickens, alive or dead, being smuggled in from a nearby farm, to the bedrooms where they were cooked. On one occasion a cormorant was boiling away in a bedroom cooking pot!

There was a lovely old lady, Everyone's Favourite Granny. She was wrinkled and tooth-less and full of fun. The Vietnamese could teach us a lesson in their love and respect for their grandparents. She was a kind of universal granny. We became so accustomed to our Vietnamese friends, with their dark, glossy hair, brown eyes and lovely smiles, that English people looked strange when we left the centre.

Apparently, because we drank milk, we smelt terrible to them and for us the whole place reeked of Chinese cooking. The Vietnamese were unaccustomed to lavatories and had to learn by diagrams that you did not stand on them or jump on them (or off them) but sat neatly upon them. The ancient plumbing systems invariably broke down when rice was shoved down the loos.

Thorney Island is heavily haunted and the Vietnamese wanted to sleep all night with the lights on ... Our ghosts were dead airmen and the Sergeant Major on the drill square up by the Guardhouse, who could be seen on moonlit nights, barking out orders to ghostly squaddies.

Across the sea, Chidham church was just visible and violent fields of mustard or rape lit up the landscape and the eerie cries of seabirds added to the beauty of the scene. For the Vietnamese and for ourselves, it was a unique two years in an island of unsurpassing beauty.

Daphne Byrne, British Council for Aid to Refugees
with the Vietnamese refugees at Thorney Island, 1979-81

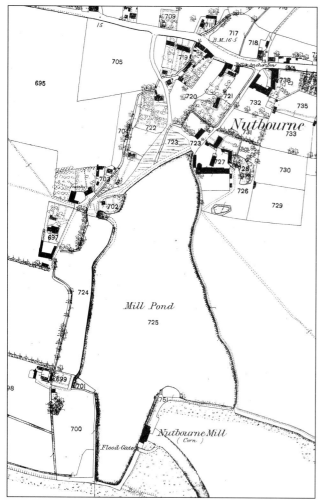

68   Nutbourne in 1875. Nutbourne Mill, a harbourside tide mill, is clearly shown with its adjacent hard where shipping once docked. (From Ordnance Survey 25" map, surveyed 1875.)

confirm the picture given by the Hearth Tax that no one in the hamlet was rich. The two largest inventories seem to be those of the husbandman John Adams, who, at his death in 1709, left goods worth £97, and of the mariner William Arney, who passed on in 1694 with some £88 to his credit.

Prinsted takes its name from the presence at one time of a pear orchard. In the Middle Ages it was never even a sub-manor, although from 1260 to 1305 there seems to have been an attempt by the Faulkner family to achieve this status. John Faulkner, lord of Wade in Warblington parish, was the favourite clerk of Henry III, who, as 'Clerk of the Hanaper', virtually acted as the keeper of the king's privy purse. In 1267, for example, he paid out over £1,200 for the rebuilding of Westminster Abbey. By 1260, in addition to Wade, he also possessed land in Prinsted; he wanted more, so in 1271 Henry III made the French abbot of Troarn give his lands at Eastoke in Hayling Island to John Faulkner, who had also now been given the royal lands there. Unfortunately for John, Henry III died in 1272; Edward I did not approve of money-grubbing clerics. By 1275 John was in disgrace, and by 1279 was dead. His brother William, and after him William's son, John II, inherited all his lands. When John II died in 1305 he was said to hold in Prinsted 'a house and barn and 60 acres of land' by service of paying 10s. yearly at the lord's court at Westbourne. His lands in Hampshire, and the services he paid, are given in full in the Inquests Post-Mortem. They include some 450 acres in Hayling Island, 128 of which were held of William Danvers 'by service of a clove-gillyflower [a carnation] yearly'. His heir was his daughter, Joan, who had married into the Botiller family of Farlington, so any dream which Henry III's clerk had of founding an important landed family came to nothing.

In the Sussex Hearth Tax the return for Prinsted is clear: there were 26 paying households, most with two or three hearths. Sarah Godfrey, however, was taxed on five, making her rich. When she died in 1674 her goods and chattels were worth over £488. There were three other households too poor to pay, so the total population of the hamlet in 1670 was probably about 130. As with Nutbourne, later population figures merge into those for Westbourne. During the 18th and 19th centuries the inhabitants of Prinsted also seem to have been engaged in corn growing. There was no mill in the hamlet, but there was a landing on Prinsted spit, where today there are two small boatyards. Here barges could come ashore and load grain to be taken for grinding at the Slipper or Nutbourne mills. Today the core of the old hamlet survives

69   Nutbourne embankment at the head of Thorney Channel in about 1919.

in a small group of houses around the old square—a rural gem—many dating from the 17th or 18th centuries.

The Hermitage owes its name to one Simon Cotes who, living in the reign of Henry VIII, built a bridge and a causeway over the Ems, probably to the north of the modern crossing. He called himself an 'Ermyt', collecting money for building a chapel where travellers along the south coast could rest, or pray, for a safe journey. From the 17th century onwards the Hermitage seems to have become increasingly important as a suburb of the growing port of Emsworth, especially after Thomas Hendy built his quay and the Slipper Mill. The Westbourne probate records include a small number for people who lived at the Hermitage. None was very wealthy and one gets the impression that this was the rougher end of the harbour for which the Emsworth constable had no jurisdiction, and Westbourne was too far away. In 1704 John Barrow, mariner, died at the Hermitage leaving goods worth only £9, and in 1719 William Rice, also of the Hermitage, died leaving £11. The latter seems to have been the proprietor of an ale-house of the lowest kind, with household goods worth just over £2 and '5 casks of beer' worth £4 15s. He had a collection of drinking vessels, including a single glass, eight chairs in his tap room and outside in the garden 'nine pins and bowles' worth 5s. It would seem likely that at this time the bridge built by Simon Cotes no longer existed and one crossed the Ems at this point by 'Stakes Ford'. It would be necessary to wait a while for the tide to fall before being able to cross, hence the need for an inn at this point. By the second half of the 18th century the work of Thomas Hendy, in establishing his quay and the Slipper millpond, and the coming of the turnpike in the 1760s, had brought a proper bridge and the traveller could pass dry-shod.

Westbourne, though not on the harbour, was an important market village until the late 18th century. In the earlier period it was a more important place than Emsworth which overtook it in the mid-18th century when Emsworth shipping and milling developed. Dallaway in

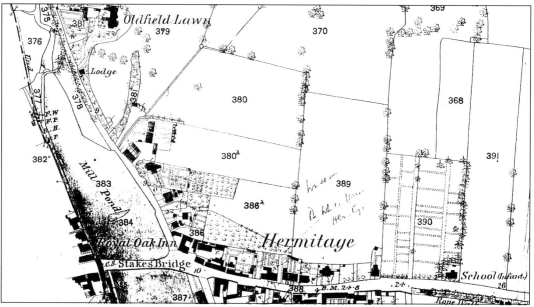

Hermitage—the Sussex-Hampshire bridge-link over the Ems.
70 *(top)   From a drawing of 1801.*
71 *(bottom)   From Ordnance Survey 25″ map, surveyed 1874.*

1815, and Horsfield in 1835, both comment on the one-time former importance of the village, the parish as a whole containing some 4,500 acres, mostly divided into small farms either held of the local lord or freehold. The soil in the south is brickearth, but in the north, on what was once Hambrook Common, enclosed from 1820 onwards, there are large deposits of gravel. In the 18th century Westbourne contained a tannery, a mill for corn, and in 1725 one for paper-making owned by Richard Clarke. There were also merchants and other tradesmen, making it a minor industrial centre in 18th-century terms, but the main occupation of all the inhabitants of the parish was agriculture. During the 19th century the population rose from 1,549 to 2,269, but the highest figure of the century was 2,450 in 1881.

X

Of Ships and Boats

Before the present century the greater part of the coastal shipping which used Chichester and the other harbours around the coasts of Great Britain was made up of wooden sailing vessels of less than 100 registered tons. Very many were employed, and it was not unusual to see fleets of several hundred small ships, collier brigs, schooners, ketches and barges waiting off the Nore for the tide to turn and carry them up the river to the Port of London. This great number of vessels required constant repair and replacement, even though an individual craft might remain in service for many years. For this reason there were small shipyards building and maintaining little ships for both the coastal trade and the fishing industry all around the coast. At various times in the 18th and 19th centuries there were shipyards around the harbour at Itchenor, Bosham and Emsworth.

In 1698 the Navy Board, which was responsible for the construction of ships for the fleet, surveyed Chichester Harbour, but said that it was 'too dangerous to enter and no fit place for a Naval establishment'. At that time the entrance was barely a quarter of a mile wide, the sand banks at the mouth were constantly shifting, and one suspects that the bar probably had less water over it than there is today, and that it shifted periodically. By the 19th century local directories were all firmly of the opinion that 'at spring tides there is a depth of 14 feet over the bar', whilst the Admiralty chart for 1845 shows a sounding of just two feet at places at Mean Low Winter Springs. Entry to the harbour, even for the sort of small vessels which traded to Dell Quay and Emsworth, seems to have been possible only from half-tide onwards, and a pilot was always needed, except for locally-owned craft. From MacKenzie's survey of 1783, when East Head reached to within 400 yards of the Hayling shore, until 1926 when the spit had almost reached its present position, the entrance seems to have become wider. Today the Conservancy constantly monitors the depth over the bar and has in the past dredged to maintain a minimum depth of 1.5 metres below chart datum. Thus it is probable that the depth over the bar is greater now than it was a century ago, despite which unwary yachtsmen still manage to run aground on the Winner on a falling tide.

There are frequent mentions of 'fisheries' in the harbour from Saxon times onwards, so one must assume that fishing boats, as well as small traders, would have been built long before the 17th century when the earliest references to ship-building on the harbour are found. On 13 August 1694 an inventory of all the goods and chattels of John Chatfield, shipwright of Itchenor, was taken by John Smith and John Day. They appraised the value at £45 10s.; this included £8 'as due from William Castellow for shipwright work done to his hoy'. A hoy was a small tubby vessel with a single mast used for local trading, and John Chatfield was probably more a ship-repairer than a ship-builder. The name John Smith is interesting, as John Smith, shipwright of Emsworth, died in 1700, and it is not impossible that he had been called in as the expert to assess the shipwright side of the business.

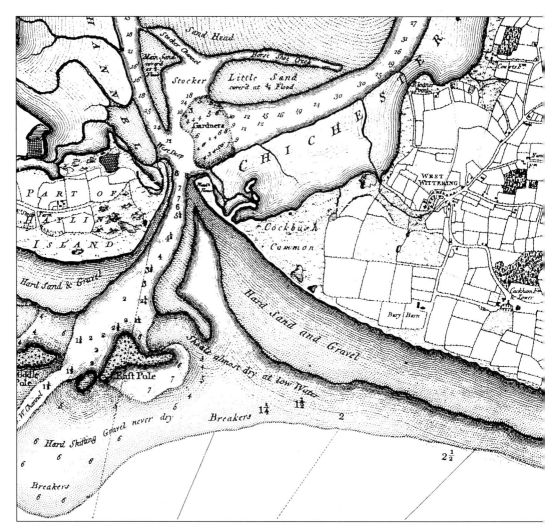

72   *Chichester Harbour: the mouth in 1778. The narrow mouth over the bar and the shifting sandbanks made navigation hazardous. The depths of water are based on Brett's survey of 1759. (From Yeakell and Gardner 2" map, 1778.)*

Only the Royal Navy and the East India Company built ships of much more than 500 tons. Surprisingly, in view of their earlier remarks, the Navy Board seems to have sanctioned the building of a number of small to medium-sized warships during the 18th and early 19th centuries, whilst at least two East Indiamen were also built here. The site was at Itchenor, the builders Vernon and Chitty, but where the yard was situated nobody knows, although saw pits and the remains of a forge have been found to the west of The Street, behind Haines' boatyard. The vessels were the *Hornet*, a sloop of 272 tons and 24 guns in 1745; the *Arundel* frigate of 509 tons and 24 guns in 1746; 1747 saw the launch of the large frigate *Penzance* of 823 tons and 44 guns, whilst the *Hind* of 510 tons and 24 guns ended the run in 1749. More ships were built between 1784 and 1810. These included the *Chichester* of 902 tons, the largest vessel ever built on the shores of the harbour. It would appear likely that all the larger vessels were taken out of the harbour 'light' after launching on the first suitable tide, to be completed at Portsmouth or Shoreham.

73   Itchenor waterfront in 1803. Warships and East Indiamen were built here on the shores of the harbour in the 18th century.

Something seems to have gone wrong at the launch of the *Chichester*, as in 1835 Horsfield wrote that:

> About half a century ago, some gentlemen of the name of Taylor, from London, attempted to establish a dock-yard for the building of ships, at Itchenor, and one of large dimensions was accordingly built; but, an accident happening at the launch, the scheme was unfortunately frustrated.

As the *Chichester* was launched on 10 March 1785 the dates match, but we cannot prove that this was the vessel he meant; significantly, subsequent naval vessels built at Itchenor—the gun-brig *Richmond* of 183 tons in 1806 and the *Pelorus* brig-sloop of 385 tons in 1808—were considerably smaller. Perhaps the most interesting vessel ever built at Itchenor was the *Transit*. Of 200 tons, and with a length of 101 feet, she was launched in May 1800. Her designer, R.H. Gower, expected her to be extremely fast but, when neither the Admiralty nor the East India Company appeared interested, she was sent to trade in the Mediterranean and was finally lost there in 1810.

During the whole of the period when a shipyard at Itchenor constructed ships of some size, the local population seems to have been about 100 at the earliest date, and no more than 170 at the later time, so workmen must have been brought in and lodged in tents or barns whilst the work was carried on. There is, as already mentioned, some evidence of boat-building at Itchenor in 1820 and in the mid-19th century, but not until Haines' yard developed from about 1912 to serve the needs of Itchenor yachtsmen does there seem to have been a permanent facility.

The story of ship- and boat-building at Bosham in the 19th century is really the story of the Apps family. William Apps, the first occupier of the Quay Meadow Shipyard, was born at Sidlesham in June 1777, the son of the baker Henry Apps. In 1798 William married Sarah Goldring at Sidlesham church. A daughter, Mary, was born in 1801, if her age of 50 given in the Bosham 1851 census is correct, when she was acting as her father's housekeeper. In 1804 a son, also

74   Transit. *Built at Itchenor and launched in 1800. She was revolutionary in her hull and rig, anticipating the lines of the 19th-century clippers by fifty years.*

called William, was born at Bosham and a second son, Thomas, was christened there in 1806 which would suggest that some sort of boatyard had already been established. By 1820 another Thomas Apps, 'the Elder', had come to live in Bosham; he too was a shipwright and may well have been William senior's brother.

In 1840, when William senior seems to have retired from the business in favour of Thomas 'the Elder', William junior, then 36 married a widow of 47, Sally Gauntlett, who owned the local grocer's shop in Bosham. It is possible that William junior, by trade a shipwright but also a ship-owner, and by virtue of his wife's enterprises often described in local directories as also a grocer, draper or merchant, had decided to leave the yard, but he had scarcely been married before both Thomas 'the Elder', and his son, also Thomas, died, and William junior took over, sending to Sidlesham for more Apps' reinforcements in the shape of John Apps' two sons, George aged 25, and James aged 20, both shown in the 1841 census as shipwrights working at Bosham. William junior's brother, Thomas, was also living there; he was a carpenter by trade, had married a Mary Anne Read in 1832 and by her was to have 11 children before her death in 1852.

William Apps senior died in 1854 owning a number of small vessels. It needs to be mentioned here that the purpose of these small local yards was as much to maintain and build vessels for the owner as it was to build for sale to other merchants. None of William Apps' vessels was very large. In 1842 he is said to have owned a half share in the ketch *William and George*, an oyster smack of 25 tons, and a further half share in the barge *Sally* of the same tonnage. In 1845 he had an interest in another ketch called the *Eliza*. In 1837 Thomas Apps, presumably 'the Elder', had owned the sloop *Prosperous*, also of 25 tons. F.D. Heneghan in his monograph *The Chichester Canal* details some 50 vessels using the Port of Chichester between 1837 and 1852; none was over 170 tons and most under 50. It is unlikely that any vessel built at Quay Meadow exceeded the larger tonnage. The yard comprised a single slip with a shed to the north where small boats were built and timber was prepared. That the enterprise was a small one may be gauged from the fact that in 1871 William Apps junior is said to have employed four men and two boys at the yard.

William junior died in 1879. Marrying late he had had no children, but his sister, Mary Smart, had a son called Thomas, and eight of Thomas the carpenter's children were alive in 1879. William Apps left the shipyard and malthouse to Thomas junior, the eldest surviving son of Thomas the carpenter, leaving money in trust for the remaining children. To Thomas Smart, said to have been born in Lewes in 1830, but of whose father no mention can be found in the

Bosham records, William left his shares in two small vessels, as well as the *William and George* already mentioned, and a schooner called the *Oak*. Thomas Smart had married an Emily Richardson some time before 1860 when their first child was baptised in Bosham church. In 1852, when aged 22, he is said to have owned a cutter of 17 tons called the *Neptune*. She may well have been an oyster smack as the Richardsons were oyster merchants. In 1871 Thomas Smart and his family were living on the 'High Path' where Thomas was running a small shipyard which may have once been the property of his late father-in-law. The widow Richardson lived in the house as head of the family and Henry Richardson, Emily's brother the oyster merchant, lived next door. There seems to have been some mystery about Thomas Smart's birth, as he was apparently never baptised, until in May 1862 he was officially received into the church in an adult christening at Bosham. Like that of William Apps in 1871, his yard also employed four men and two boys. He was not just a small ship/boat-builder but also a merchant. From 1864 he had owned a vessel called the *Busy Bee* which traded to Sunderland for coal, making some six return voyages a year. In 1890, four years before his death in 1894, she was sold to an Irish owner and eventually scrapped in 1912. If Thomas Smart had built her, and there is some reason to believe that he had, she is a tribute to his skill as a shipwright. Two other vessels built by Smart were the *Lady of the Lake* of 84 tons, also used on the Sunderland run, and the *Dolly Varden*. After Smart's death his widow kept on the yard which was run for her by Thomas Apps' younger brother and Smart's cousin, Abraham Apps. Abraham seems to have run it until the 1920s. He died aged 80 in 1927, and thereafter it seems to have been known as Scovell's yard.

When Thomas Apps took over at Quay Meadow in 1879 he already owned ships and property, and ran several businesses in Bosham. Perhaps he neglected the yard, for in 1881 he was said to employ there only one man and a boy. One of his interests was the *Hope* of 143 tons, also employed in the coal trade; he sold her to a Frenchman in 1902 when his new ketch, the *Good Hope* of 76 tons, was launched. She was the last sailing coaster to be built at Bosham, for by then the age of such ships was drawing to a close. Thomas Apps died in 1912, his widow in

75 Apps' Shipyard, Bosham, in 1901. On the stocks is the Good Hope, *the last sailing coaster built at Bosham.*

76   New Prince of Wales. *This Southend-based passenger ferry was built at Bosham in 1922-3.*

1917. A house called 'The Slip' was built on the slipway site. The land on which the yard was situated seems to have been leased from the manor of Bosham, and by 1924 this lease had lapsed. When Lord Iveagh acquired the estate in 1924 he leased what remained of the old shipyard to Spencer and Bryce who used the Apps' shed to build dinghies and small craft until the outbreak of war in 1939 when the yard closed.

In the early years of the present century Alex Fowler established what later became known as Mariner's Shipyard at the eastern end of the Trippit; by 1907 it appeared in *Kelly's Directory*. The shed, in which in 1922-3 he built the *New Prince of Wales* for the Southend Navigation Company, is said to have been built during the 1914-18 war, so he may well have been engaged in work for the Admiralty during that period. When launched, the *New Prince of Wales*, at 108 feet long, was said to be the largest flat-bottomed passenger ferry in the world, but the work seems to have been too much for the firm. Fowler was declared bankrupt and the shed and equipment were auctioned off, to be bought by Colonel F.S. Burne. Burne also bought more land at the site of the now defunct Burne's Shipyard, and for the next 18 years he built many small sailing craft and racing dinghies. These were to be the most numerous craft in the harbour once the old industries of coastal trading and fishing had declined. Much of the work took the form of *12 ft National Dinghies*, but in 1938 Burne designed and built the first of the *Chichester 18 ft One Design Yachts*. The war then intervened and in 1945 Colonel Burne sold out, the yard coming into the hands of R.M. & D.G. Bowker in 1947. At first it was repairs and maintenance, then in 1950 R.M. Bowker left the partnership, D.G. Bowker sold the Mariner's shed, bought more land at the present Burne's site and began the construction of racing yachts which was to last until he sold the yard in 1967. In all some 60 *South Coast One Design* boats were built, together with a number of cruising yachts, *Dragons, X-Class* and *5.5 metres*. Included in the latter class was *Vision* which D.G. Bowker took to the Melbourne Olympics in 1956 and which was awarded the silver medal for her class. When D.G. Bowker sold Burne's he was employing some 40 hands, but in an age when skill is no longer at a premium there is no longer much scope for the craftsmanship in wood and the traditional ways of the shipwright. Burne's finally closed in 1985, and the yard is now derelict. The shed at Mariner's burned down in the '60s. Today no vessel is either built or repaired in Bosham village, and the site of the old Mariner's yard is now occupied by houses.

The original shipyard at Emsworth was on the Westbrook, probably between what are now School Lane and Nile Street; John Smith and his son, also John, were there in the latter part of the 17th century and the first half of the 18th, but in about 1750 the Westbrook was walled off by an embankment—or bund—to form a tidal millpond, so it was necessary to find an alternative site for a shipyard. Land at Sweare Lane—now King Street—was bought; a new yard was opened by the shipwright George Norris and his young partner John King and is said to have been in use by 1755.

One of the problems facing the local historian is to distinguish between various persons with the same name; in the second half of the 18th century there were too many John Kings living in Emsworth! The John King of the shipyard, like Joseph before him, is said to have come from Titchfield and also married a cousin—although there may be a degree of confusion in the legend—in this case an Elizabeth King. The marriage took place in 1761 when John King is thought to have been 26 and Elizabeth was 23 years old. John King, 'Shipbuilder', has gone down in legend in Emsworth and many tales are told of his actions. John King I died in 1800 and a second John King took over the yard, but as far as legend is concerned there seems to have been only ONE John King for the whole of the period covered by the wars with France from 1793-1815. John King's partner, George Norris, died in 1805. Described as a shipwright, he was probably the practical man to John King I's business brain.

Little is known of the type or size of ship built at the yard during the early period, but a list of half a dozen vessels said to have been built at Emsworth between 1784 and 1805 shows only two between 100 and 200 tons; the other four were smaller. During the French wars the basic work of the yard was probably the construction of ships' boats and launches, together with ash-turning, making boathooks, pike staves and capstan bars. The original yard was twice the size of the later Emsworth shipyard for reasons given below. In 1795 a John King, probably the first of the name, is said to have built the house called 'The Hut' in King Street in the course of a single summer day. One suspects that the chimney breasts had already been built in brick, whilst the wooden frames prefabricated in the yard were merely assembled, but it makes a good story. On John I's death he left his personal property to his widow Elizabeth for her life, to be divided on her death equally between his children, 'share and share alike'. There is no mention as to what was to become of the yard. We know that he left seven daughters and that a son called William died in infancy; what we do NOT know is the relationship between him and John King 'Junior' who appears to have taken over the yard. On the latter's death in 1827 he was said to have been 70 years old, which implies that he was born in 1757 before the marriage of John I to Elizabeth in January 1761. It is just possible that he was the son of John I by a previous unrecorded marriage, or that he was actually born in January 1762, and the birth was not entered in the Warblington register. The first birth of a daughter to John and Elizabeth was January 1763, so this is possible and the age in the burial register may be incorrect. In the 1790s, when he was licensee of the *Crown Inn*, John II is called 'John King Junior', John I being John King Senior', so there does seem to be an implied relationship.

With the end of the French wars it is likely that work at the yard declined. In the 1823 directory it appears that the western part was now purely a timber yard run by John King II's son, John King III, whilst the eastern half carried on ship- and boat-building under the guidance of his younger brother, William King. John King III died in 1857; his widow Jane carried on the timber business until the late 1870s when her son William II took over. The latter predeceased his mother, dying in 1884, the last male in the line of King ship-builders, for William King I had died in 1844 without a male heir and the yard had passed out of the family's possession. From 1844 to 1855 the owner was David Palmer Walker, of an old established Emsworth family. Longcroft says he built a vessel of some 400 tons, but there is no real evidence for this in the Portsmouth Port Books. The next owner was William Foster. He bought the yard to be able to maintain his small fleet of coastal traders, and to build for himself and for sale.

Today, when ships of 10,000 tons are small, we tend to forget how tiny were the vessels with crews of six or seven, which even a century ago made long and arduous voyages as a matter of course. In 1873, to quote one example, the *Thorney Island* built at Emsworth, and part owned by W. Foster, though her principal shareholders lived in Portsmouth, made a voyage to the port of Archangel on the White Sea. Sailing in May they found the port still ice-bound when they reached it in June, and could only enter at the end of that month. They shipped a cargo, but when they came to leave another vessel dragged her anchor, hit the *Thorney Island*, damaged the bulwarks and carried away most of the standing rigging. John Steel, master of the seven-man crew, commented in his log that they had 'made good the damage'. By September the vessel had returned safely to Portsmouth.

W. Foster was, amongst other trades, a coal merchant. One of his vessels, the *Indian Queen*, made regular voyages to Sunderland, not always without adventure. In December 1874 she stranded at Whitby, but was got off successfully; in 1893 luck ran the other way when she was lost with all hands off the Farne Islands. William Foster had a large family: the two most important of his sons were John Duncan, born in 1858, and Walter, born in 1862. The former became both a ship-owner and a ship-designer, but the story of his life and work belongs in the next chapter. Walter took over his father's timber and coal business when the latter died.

William Foster was a businessman, not a shipwright. During his time as the owner of the yard, the construction of vessels appears to have been the responsibility of Joseph Edgar, the foreman shipwright, and his sons. By the mid-1870s Joseph had retired and Foster brought in George Apps the younger, son of George Apps, shipwright of Bosham, the

77 Indian Queen. *Part of Foster's Emsworth fleet in the 19th century.*

cousin of Thomas Apps. By 1881 George had been joined by his younger brother, Albert. The relationship between William Foster and the Apps brothers is obscure. When the barge *Champion* was built at the Emsworth shipyard in 1880 it was said to have been the work of George Apps. After the death of William Foster it was Albert Apps who figured as the builder, and he seems by then to have been the owner, responsible for building a number of barges for the Littles of Langstone, but increasingly turning to the building and maintenance of the large yachts then so fashionable. By 1914 it was no longer 'Apps' Yard' but 'Emsworth Shipyard', a name it kept until the 1970s when it reverted briefly to being the 'John King Shipyard'. The building and maintenance of leisure craft continued at Emsworth throughout the 1920s and 1930s, was interrupted by the last war when small naval assault craft were built and maintained, and continued thereafter until the 1970s when such work became increasingly unprofitable owing to the development of

78 (above)   Emsworth Shipyard in the 1920s.

79 (right)   Boat-builders at Hayling in the 1930s. At Sparkes' yard, Hayling Island. Believed to be Ned Sparkes (left) in conversation with John Haines from the Itchenor yard.

glass-fibre hulls cast in moulds, rather than built of wood by skilled craftsmen. By the 1980s the yard had closed. Today the whole of the area which once formed the shipyard founded by Norris and King in the 1750s has been given over to housing. Another closure, in 1971, was the boat-building firm of J.G. Parham and Son which had been at Dolphin Quay since the 1930s. Now no further ship- or boat-building is carried on at Emsworth itself.

As coastal trade declined in the late 1920s and '30s leisure activities took over the harbour and, to service the yachts and dinghies, further yards were established away from the old centres of Bosham and Emsworth. In 1937 the first marina was developed in Birdham Pool, for the tide mill had closed two years earlier. It had its own small yard to service boats kept there. Just before this event, in 1935, two new yards were opened on Hayling Island. These were Sparkes' yard, off Eastoke, and the Hayling Yacht Company on Mill Rythe. Contemporary with these was Combes' yard on Bosham Hoe. Sparkes' yard was to specialise in the building of fast motor boats, the Yacht Company being more interested in sailing craft construction. The final pre-war development was the Itchenor Shipyard, started in about 1936 and enlarged in 1938; it was designed to specialise in the building of fast motor cruisers. All these works were taken over by the Admiralty during the last war, their activities being described in chapter XIII.

After 1945-6 all the yards were able to return to their original use, the construction of pleasure and leisure craft. The most successful is now called the Northshore Yard. Today based at Itchenor, it was formed in 1971 at the old Emsworth Yard, moving to Itchenor two years later when the buildings at Emsworth were sold. It is today the only yard on the harbour regularly building and fitting out yachts and uses glass reinforced plastic hulls moulded at its Havant factory. The remainder all carry out maintenance of existing vessels, but could build to order if required. Haines' Yard at Itchenor and Combes' Yard at Bosham specialise in wooden hulls, the last in the harbour to do so. Haines' also provides services for the boats of the Itchenor Sailing Club, and there are the two small yards at Prinsted, Andrew's and Payne's, the latter specialising in 'self-help' refits.

Since the first marina was opened at Birdham, three more marinas have been developed on the harbour. They are the Chichester Yacht Basin, situated near the old Chichester Canal on what was once the old Saltern, Northney Marina in the north of Hayling Island, and the Tarquin Yacht Harbour at the Hermitage side of Emsworth Channel. All provide services for those with marina berths.

Combes Boatyard
SPECIALISTS IN WOODEN BOATS
REPAIR & RESTORATION
WINTER STORAGE — 60 TON SLIPWAY
HARDWOODS & PLY TRADITIONAL FASTENINGS
PAINT VARNISH & ADHESIVES
ENGINEERING
TEL 0243 573194   FAX 0243 573827

80/81   Repair work at Combes' Boatyard, Bosham. David Bishop at work on Vagabond, *1995. With Haines at Itchenor this is one of the last specialists in wooden boats in the harbour.*

XI

Of Fish, Fishermen and Smugglers

One factor which made the harbour so important for those who lived on its shores was the great number and variety of fish found both within the entrance and along the adjacent coasts. Historically the most important catch was the oyster. Originally plentiful, by the early 19th century the local beds had been largely fished-out and new sources were required. Then in the 1830s an extremely rich, and hitherto unknown, bed was discovered off Shoreham, and similar beds were found off the French coast; the oyster trade was saved. In addition to oysters, other molluscs—cockles, mussels and winkles—were always in good supply. Scallops could be dredged in the Channel and crabs and lobsters trapped in pots moored offshore.

82   Decaying oyster coves at Emsworth. A relic of the Emsworth oyster trade, photographed in 1995.

Charles Longcroft, writing in the 1850s, gave a comprehensive survey of all the fish found locally. These included plaice, flounder and sole, whiting and whiting-pout, all found in abundance. Outside the harbour there was bass, skate or conger eel and occasionally cod, and in the streams flowing into the harbour were trout and eels. From July to September great shoals of mackerel appeared in Hayling Bay and off the Witterings, to be followed from Michaelmas to the year's end by herring. Another fish, considered to be a luxury in the Middle Ages, was grey mullet, still plentiful today. In early times they were often held captive in ponds dug along the shore, to be a ready source of fish for church-inspired fast days.

Somewhat surprisingly the references to fisheries in Domesday Book show that locally the value was small: two at Bosham were worth only 8s. 10d., and two at Hayling just 20d. Throughout history the normal pattern of fishing appears to have been wet fish in the summer and shell-fish in the winter. Oysters were dredged up, and in the 19th century were put into the wet-wells of fishing smacks or into the tubs of saltwater aboard smaller vessels. They were then laid down in coves—man-made holding ponds—on the foreshore at Emsworth, Bosham or at Hayling, and lifted, as convenient, for sale.

In the Middle Ages the chief problem for fishermen was how to keep the catch fresh. Long voyages were out of the question, so fish was either eaten quickly after being caught, or else salted, smoked or pickled in brine. One would have thought that, with so much fish locally available, little would have been brought in from elsewhere, yet in the 17th century considerable quantities of both salt cod and pickled herrings were imported through Dell Quay. By then, of course, the ritual of 'fish days' was not as strict as it had been. Even so it is surprising that, when Roy Morgan made his survey of over 2,000 17th-century inhabitants of Chichester, he only found two fishmongers, compared with 124 butchers, perhaps indicating that little fish was actually being eaten.

We know that men fished the harbour in the Middle Ages, as there are many records of dues being paid to local landlords. Indeed the prebendal rector of Thorney managed to collect a tithe of fish; there is also a reference to a 'fishery of captive mullet' at Warblington in the late 15th century. What we do not know is whether local boats were sound enough to fish far out to sea, and it is only when probate records of the 16th century become available that we start to discover whether the fishermen were rich or poor, and about the tools of their trade. The earliest such record is probably that of Philip Hewitt of Emsworth, who died in 1596; his 'goods and chattels' were valued at £22 15s. 3d. and included 'A half share in a boat and dredge' worth 20s. and a 'fishing nett' worth the same sum. The dredge would indicate that part of his catch was oysters. Another early record is of the Frogbrook family of Bosham, active in the oyster trade in the early 17th century, whilst in 1671 William Spriggs of Emsworth, fisherman, died owning:

> A Hoy and two small boats with other
> fishing craft such as nets and draggs   -   Valued at £30.

That he had a hoy is a good indication that he could, and did, fish outside the harbour.

William Spriggs and some of the other Emsworth fishing families were wealthy men, the Holloways (already mentioned) particularly so. We must assume that they were 'the money'd men' of Emsworth whom Defoe said established the trade in corn from Chichester to London in association with the merchants and maltsters of the former city, some time around 1700. Men such as the Mansers and Hedgers of Emsworth seem to have fished full time, with perhaps a little local trade thrown in; there is no suggestion in their inventories of any alternative employment. There were others on the harbour who obviously farmed as well as fished, living lives not dissimilar to those of 18th-century Scottish crofters. Thus Robert Coombes, fisherman of West Wittering, on his death in 1621, possessed '6 acres of land' planted with crops, 'worth £4' as well as a half share in 'an old boat with anchor and dragge' worth 11s., whilst Edward Rowlands of Emsworth in 1677 owned 'one old boat and all belonging to her' worth 10s., together with '3 acres of corn in the Common Field' worth £3.

Not all local fishermen were as fortunate as those of Emsworth. In March 1677 John Holbrooke, fisherman of New Fishbourne, died in debt, having borrowed money from a number of richer local men. His estate was worth just £13 12s., his debts amounting to £12 14s. 10d. The principal creditor, Charles Ballow, took charge of the appraisal of the goods, taking care to recover his share of the debt, and to settle the others. John Holbrooke's unfortunate son and heir received just 17s. 2d., not much to start a new career when his father's boat has gone to pay off his debts.

When Dallaway wrote in 1815 he was clear that fishing at Bosham was very important. In 1817 when Butler listed the numbers of boats in the harbour, he put Emsworth just ahead of Bosham. Then in the 1820s new oyster beds were found and oystermen from both sides of the Channel flocked to harvest this bonanza. At this time there seems to have been no regulation on the dredging of oysters; men dredged as they wished, although, if the oysters were unfit due to the spring spawning, careful fishermen left them alone. In the late

---

The Bosham Dredgermen's Co-operative Society Limited

Report
For the year ending 31st August 1894

The sale of Oysters has, we are glad to say, still further advanced this year; but the price had been low in consequence of their being, comparatively, but poorly fished.

The upper grounds during last summer became covered with a marine growth which accumulated mud to such an extent as to completely smother the oysters laid in the upper reaches. Notwithstanding the cleaning in the previous spring (1893) and subsequent working on the ground, it continued through the following winter and threatened to do considerable damage. It has, however, we are happy to say, succumbed to the continual working this summer; and the grounds are now clean throughout.

We consider the prospects of the Fishery are good, for the accumulation of Indigenous oysters since 1890 must be considerable. A small fall of spat is noticed.

John Smith, Chairman
F.W. Jarrad, Managing Director

1830s, when the bulk of the Channel oyster fishery was shared by both British and French fishermen, the government of Louis Philippe decided that regulations were required. In 1843 both countries signed a convention which prohibited the dredging of oysters between 1 May and 30 September—the rules about only eating oysters when there is an R in the month had been finalised. The success of the south coast oystermen with their new sources of supply seems to have upset the men of Whitstable and they obtained legislation to regulate the industry which, according to Henry Cheal in his book *The Ships and Mariners of Shoreham*, 'did much to cripple the trade at Shoreham, Havant, Emsworth, and Bosham'. If parliament could regulate the oyster industry, it could also legislate to allow the oystermen to regulate themselves. In 1871 the men of Emsworth obtained the first Emsworth Fishery Order which gave them certain rights and protection from fishermen from elsewhere, and in 1880 the men of Bosham were able to form their own Dredgermen's Co-operative Society. Today the fishery on the

83   *Packing oysters at Bosham Quay earlier this century.*

84   *Emsworth fishermen in about 1902. The craft are inshore fishing boats known as jerkies.*

Hampshire side is governed by the Emsworth Fishermen's Federation controlling the northern end of Emsworth Channel, whilst the rest of the harbour is an open fishery.

It is perhaps necessary to point out that by the 19th century there were two distinct classes of fishermen in the harbour. Firstly there were the men who fished inshore. Their craft were small so they were rarely away from home for more than a day at a time. More important, though less numerous, were the men who, in addition to some inshore fishing, crewed the smacks. These vessels, which varied in size from cutters of some 25 tons to ketches of over 50 tons, could be away from their home port for up to a month at a time. At Emsworth at the turn of the century, when J.D. Foster's smacks were based at Newhaven, it seems to have been the custom for the crew to spend three weeks at sea and a week back home before embarking on their next voyage. Details of the smacks and their crews can be found in the records of the Port of Portsmouth in the Portsmouth City Records Office, but there are almost no records about the much smaller boats of the inshore fishermen. By the turn of the century at Bosham the standard inshore boat was the open Bosham punt with its single mast and dipping lugsail. Here there seem to have been fewer smacks than at Emsworth, but a greater number of small fishing boats.

Fishing Boat Statistics, 1817

Eastern Harbour

Emsworth	30	Fishbourne	3
Prinsted & Nutbourn	3	Dell Quay	3
Thorney Island	1	Birdham	3
Chidham	1	Itchenor	2
Bosham	25	West Wittering	10

Western Harbour

Langstone	5	Kingston	12
Hayling North	6	Shut	5
Sinar	12	Bedhampton	7

Walter Butler, *Topographical Account of the Hundred of Bosmere, in Hampshire ...* (1817)

The Bosham smacks included the *William and George*, already mentioned, belonging first to William Apps and then to Thomas Smart. Another was the *Caroline* owned by George Woods, who was called 'barge-owner' in 1878. *Caroline* was first registered at the Port of Portsmouth in 1879, and remained the property of the Woods family until she was sunk and partially broken up in 1896. Her normal crew numbered four: master, mate and two seamen; sometimes George Woods took her out himself. Born in 1817, he was over 70 when he took his smack on a fishing trip in the Channel in 1888. Members of the Woods family always comprised at least two, and sometimes three, of the crew, and if George Woods did not skipper her himself, then a son or a brother did. Latterly, much of the time was spent 'laid up'; thus in the record for July to December 1890, and also for the following year, the entry in the report of proceedings submitted to the Marine Superintendent at Southampton is 'Vessel Laid Up during Half Year', whilst for January to June 1890 the entry was 'from January to 30 April Fishing in English Channel,

Unlawful Fishing

The fisheries are comprised in two arms of the sea, distinguished by the names of the eastern and western harbours, and were formerly of great value to those inhabitants upon the coast, who exercised the employment of fishing, and who were enabled to support their families without assistance from the parish, by the profits of their boats; but from the great destruction which of late years has been made in the brood, spawn, and fry, of fish, bred in these harbours, the fisheries are now become unprofitable, the loss of which is felt by the public, as well as the individual employed in the fishery: and for this there can be no remedy, unless the legislature passes an act to regulate the period of fishing, and the size of fish to be caught ...

The fishermen are deprived of their bread by fishing smacks from the eastern coast, which, from their size and superiority of sailing, sweep the bottom of the sea and take away every oyster, and their success encourages them to defy the native fisherman, or run down his little boat, which gets entangled with the trawling tackle of the smacks. This unlawful fishing began about twenty years ago ... each smack three or four hands on board, working six or seven drags, and catching as many tubs in a tide, each tub from six to seven hundred market oysters, or one thousand of different sizes. The smacks then drag for, and carry away all the stubs, brood, spawn, and fry, of every description, and by such close dragging the food or nutriment, as well as the protection of the infant brood, is carried away to the great injury of the oysters, and depriving them of their natural support ...

The native fishermen are, therefore, not only deprived by these intruders of their former means of subsistence, but the community are sufferers, and, in a short time, this harbour, which produced oysters of great size and flavor, will yield no profit whatever.

Oysters have been caught in the harbour 4 inches over, as broad as a biscuit; but the market oyster is 2° inches.

Walter Butler, *Topographical Account of the Hundred of Bosmere, in Hampshire* ... (1817)

since laid up', which probably means she was dredging for oysters and scallops. At only 22 tons this smack was one of the smaller deep-sea fishing vessels using the harbour.

Study of the census returns for Bosham shows that many of those living near the shore in Bosham village were listed as fishermen. They included a family with the name of Levitt, first met with as fishermen in the 18th century. In Emsworth similar returns show that in South Street and the associated courts there were also many fishermen. Most of them no doubt owned a share in one of the Emsworth jerkies—the standard Emsworth inshore boat, rather heavier than a Bosham punt, with a standing lug and foresail on the single mast—but they were also prepared to crew the oyster smacks of J.D. Foster and John Kennett.

The former was the eldest surviving son of William Foster. In the 1881 census he is called 'oyster merchant', having apparently bought the cutter *Jack Tar* from the Cribb brothers in that year. First registered in 1869, and said to be Emsworth-built but of only 15 tons, she was wrecked off Selsey that December, her crew surviving. This set-back perhaps suggested to J.D. Foster the need for his own yard and vessels built to his own specifications. In the mid-1880s he established his business in the disused malthouse on Hendy's Quay. He bought timber, and set up his own saw mill, becoming ship-builder, ship-owner, timber-merchant and a power in Emsworth until his death in 1940. The first vessel he built was the 55-ton ketch *Evolution* first registered in 1888, followed by a succession of vessels, all launched into Dolphin Lake. His second craft was the ketch *Thistle*, registered in 1889 and lost in December that year. Altogether by 1901 he had 10 smacks afloat. There were three small cutters, the *Nautilus*, *Cymba* and *Aura*, all of 22 tons and registered in 1893; in 1890 came the ketches *Sybil* and *Ostrea* of 35 tons; in 1895 two other ketches, the *Nonpareil* of 69 and the *Una* of 41 tons; in 1896 came the *Sylvia* also of 35 tons. Finally in 1901 there was the *Echo*, a steam auxiliary ketch of 52 tons; at 110 feet in length she is generally reckoned to be Foster's finest craft. By now he had perfected his designs, and his vessels with their raking clipper bows, fine lines and overhanging counters are generally said to be the finest working fishing craft ever built in English ports.

In 1901 Foster laid down a further vessel, but she was never completed because of the pollution incident in 1902 which destroyed the local oyster trade. By that time Foster's ten vessels, and John Kennett's two or three, were all working successfully out of Emsworth. Oyster smacks had wet-wells in which the shell-fish catch was kept fresh during the time

85   The Emsworth ketch, the Nonpareil *in about 1900.*

the vessel was at sea. The *Echo* could hold some 90 tons of water in her well and a series of pipes and pumps enabled the water to be continually changed. When pumped out she rose by 18 inches. The *Echo* and the larger smacks all had steam winches to help with the sails and trawl warps, but crews were small: the cutters took six men, the larger ketches eight; the *Echo* had 11 but this included two engineers. In order to have somewhere other than the foreshore coves in which to store his oysters, in about 1898 Foster built what Emsworth people later came to call the *Ark*. When she was launched from her building ramp on the shore south of Hendy's Quay she caused such a wash that many boats in the harbour were all but swamped. Worst of all she was not a success, seems never to have been used, and lay on the mud on the Sussex side of the Ems channel for 75 years before finally being broken up.

In 1901 it is recorded that as many as 576,976 oysters were taken from the coves at Bosham, and that the value of the catch was over £1,875. The oysters from Emsworth may well have been worth more as, when their sale was banned, J.D. Foster claimed that his loss was £3,000. It was said that 100,000 oysters a week passed through the Emsworth beds. In summer 1902 a new sewer was built at Emsworth. Discharging raw sewage at an outfall near the Town Quay, the effluent passed over the oyster coves. That November there was a banquet at

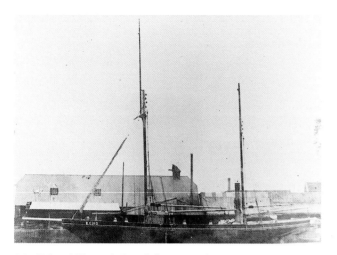

86 Echo *of Emsworth. Launched in 1901* Echo *was regarded as the queen of the Emsworth oyster fleet. Here she is seen alongside Hendy's Quay.*

Winchester followed a day later by another at Southampton, after which several guests fell ill and the dean of Winchester died. In January 1903 the local medical officer of health declared Emsworth Harbour to be polluted and the sale of Emsworth oysters was banned. Almost immediately the ban was extended to the whole of Chichester Harbour, including Bosham. The latter managed to get a clean bill of health a few years later, but the ban on Emsworth lasted until 1914 when the new sewage works was completed and only treated effluent entered the harbour. By then, of course, the war had begun and large-scale oyster farming had to wait until 1919. But as far as J.D. Foster and his crews were concerned, they could, and did, spend the winter at Newhaven and sent their cargoes of shell-fish by rail direct to London. The inshore fishermen suffered the worst hardship. During the summer when the smacks were laid up, their crews found alternative employment on the large racing yachts based at Cowes.

When the Great War was over and oyster fishing recommenced in the harbour, it was not at the same level as it had been before 1902. Foster's smacks made fewer and fewer voyages. In 1927 the *Sylvia*, on her last voyage to the French coast, was sunk by a steamer in mid-Channel and her crew lost. The two ketches run by the Kennetts continued working. There were still oysters in Emsworth-owned coves off North Hayling in 1939, but on the whole the industry throughout the harbour was but a shadow of what it had been. When war came again in 1939, this was the end. The inhabitants of Emsworth and Bosham will never again see a sailing smack coming up harbour, sails set and drawing, having crossed the bar at half flood to use the incoming tide to help her up the channel before she finally brings to at Hendy's Quay or the Raptackle. The remains of Foster's fleet have now been removed from the berths they used to occupy; the malthouse which served as his sail store and mould loft burned down in 1935. Little is left of Foster's enterprises to remind us of this today.

The harbour was not only full of fish, it was also full of fowl. The document of 1503 which referred to 'captive mullet' at Warblington also mentioned the value of wildfowling 'at a little isle called Fowlie Hill', and in the 17th and 18th centuries there are occasional references in the inventories of both Emsworth and Bosham fishermen to 'guns' or 'fowling pieces'. Thus in 1684 Richard Hedger of Emsworth had a gun, in 1714 John Levitt of Bosham had three guns, and in 1754

87 *Joseph Bethell's probate inventory of 1754. Bethell, an Emsworth seaman, had 'one sea-fowling gun' as well as a sea-chest and sea-bed, and owned a fourth part of a small boat.*

'Horsing' in the Harbour

The garfish is a lamb of the sea. He is never tired of gambolling, and this spirit of *joi de vivre* often leads to his undoing.

Garfish follow the whitebait shoals, but when not pursuing their prey they hunt around for straggling flotsam in the shape of sticks, paper bags or small pieces of wreckage on the surface; then the fun begins. Silvery bodies flash in the sunlight as they spring from side to side of any object which catches their eye. All thought of food is forgotten as they follow the floating debris, leaping, twisting and turning.

When the garfish are known to have arrived the fishermen go 'horsing'. This is a colloquial and rather obscure name for a remarkable method of reaping the harvest of the sea. The men cut branches of withy sticks, to which are tied lengths of string. These are stowed in the boat and with a seine or long net abroad the fishers set off. When the garfish are sighted the sticks are distributed over the water and kept in position by the mooring lines. Usually the anxious watchers have not long to wait before the fish indulge in their passion for gymnastics. When the performance is in full progress the net is shot and many sad and disillusioned fish appear in the market.

This interesting method has been practiced in Chichester Harbour from time immemorial.

Grey mullet are perhaps the most difficult to capture with a net. Instead of making a blind rush for the bag of the net when drawn into the shallows, they nose about in a most methodical manner, and if no outlet presents itself they leap to freedom over the cork-line like greyhounds over hurdles.

To outwit their quarry the fishermen adopt many methods. Some, when grey mullet are known to be in the net, beat the water frantically with an oar, others wade waist deep, making the welkin ring with shouts and oaths in an endeavour to prevent the fish from leaping.

But perhaps the most ingenious scheme was that of an old fisherman at Emsworth, who trained a Labrador retriever to swim constantly round the incoming net. Thus, between the net, the dog and the deep sea the mullet were forced to passive resistance.

R. Thurston Hopkins, *Small Sailing Craft* (1931)

Joseph Bethell of Emsworth, mariner, had 'one sea-fowling gun'. From the 19th century onwards the punt-gun wildfowler with his gun-punt was a common sight in the harbour. The birds are now for the most part protected and for the Brent Goose the harbour is one of the most important wintering grounds in the country. A surviving gun-punt may be seen in Havant Museum.

Perhaps one ought not to talk of smugglers in the same chapter as fishermen, but they did help the shore-based smuggling gangs, for they alone knew the beaches and harbours used to land the cargoes. In the 18th century the women of Britain had discovered the newly fashionable Chinese drink, tea. The government, always keen to raise revenue from luxuries, taxed it highly, so tea, along with 'Brandy for the Parson' and ''Baccy for the Clerk' became a staple of the smuggling trade. The area of Chichester Harbour was particularly suitable for running cargoes, and in 1750 the single customs riding officer at Emsworth pointed this out. 'Caves'

The Gunner

Towards the close of the year, when the inclemencies of the season force the water fowl into the harbour, every one is busy in arranging his sporting apparatus to attack the feathered strangers; not the severest frost or the bitterest north wind can intimidate the gunner, who watches through the night, or attends the shores regularly at day break and dusk; but the best time is twelve o'clock at night, at low water, when the birds are feeding upon the mud, which enables the gunner to crawl upon his hands and knees in search of them, directed by their cries, and carrying a mud-stock gun upon his shoulder, of ponderous weight, which generally carries five ounces of shot.

A few years ago, a fowler came from Dover, and resided with his wife and family in a little sloop, anchored off Pilsea Island; he ventured with his little boat in every situation, and explored the various fowl that frequented the coast, his boat being just sufficient to contain him at full length, and in this posture he moved himself along in every direction; his instrument of destruction was 9 feet in length, rested upon the stern of the boat, carrying a pound of shot 150 yards with certainty, and in one winter, (1789) he earned £100. The fishermen, unable to excel him, called him the Gunner; and, in summer, he used his nets with equal dexterity.

Walter Butler, *Topographical Account of the Hundred of Bosmere, in Hampshire ...* (1817)

were dug on Hayling Beach—covered holes in the dunes and shingle banks—where goods brought in could be hidden until moved by local watermen to places inland. The local centre of this trade was Rowlands Castle, where two counties and three parishes meet. It was difficult for three constables and two sets of magistrates to co-ordinate searches and captures, for no constable had power of arrest outside his parish, no magistrate outside his county.

In the 1740s, however, the real villains came from Hawkhurst in Kent. In 1747, when a cargo of tea belonging to one of their number was seized by the customs and locked in Poole Customs House, the Hawkhurst Gang organised a raid to liberate their goods using local Sussex and Hampshire men. The raid was a success, but a Poole shoemaker, Daniel Chater, recognised some of the gang and turned king's evidence. With an elderly customs officer called William Galley he was sent to swear to a warrant in front of a Sussex magistrate. They were surprised by smugglers at Rowlands Castle and later brutally murdered. The Duke of Richmond was outraged and led the campaign to root out the murderers and break up the local gangs. In this he was successful, and in January 1749 at a special assize at Chichester, seven smugglers were found guilty; six were hanged and the seventh died in gaol. Smuggling died down for a while, aided not least by the government lowering and simplifying the tariffs on imports.

By the 1780s customs duties rose again because of the war in America, and smuggling once more increased. This time the 'free-traders' had vessels which were both larger, faster, more heavily armed and carried more men than the revenue cutters. The *Roebuck*, then patrolling Chichester Harbour, was no match for them, as her captain reported to the authorities. Soldiers were brought in to help. In 1786 men from Fort Cumberland caught a gang trying to make a run into Langstone Harbour. After the American War of Independence, the Younger

Mr Galley and Mr Chater put by ye Smugglers on one Horse near Rowland Castle.
A. Steele who was Admitted a Kings Evidence. B. Little Harry. C. Jackson. D Carter.
E. Donner. F. Richards.   1. Mr Galley. 2. Mr Chater.

88   *The smugglers wreak their revenge. The terrifying ordeal of Galley and Chater near Rowlands Castle in 1748.*

Pitt, as prime minister, reduced the duties and simplified the tariffs. Once more smuggling declined, until the French wars and fresh increases in duty encouraged the local gangs, now often joined by smugglers from across the Channel, bringing in not only contraband, but spies and 'seditious literature' from revolutionary France.

At the end of the 18th century one local smuggling group was the Langstone Gang, which, as its name implies, was centred on that small hamlet. Their base was what is now the *Royal Oak* inn, then called the *Red Lion*, and they were extremely successful. When the war with France ended, the Navy took over the manning of the revenue cutters and there was a general crack-down on smuggling, almost 900 smuggling vessels being seized. The trade, however, continued, and smugglers became more daring. In the 1830s the smugglers sank huge rafts of casks beneath the waters of Langstone Harbour, as can be seen in a display at Havant Museum. In 1830 they ran a cargo of liquor worth £1,000 through Pagham, and in 1849 a consignment of tubs was seized on Cockbush Common near the harbour entrance in West Wittering parish. The coastguard service had been established in 1831, and the Snow Hill station here was one of the first to be built. Others were established at East Wittering, on Hayling Beach, and lastly at Langstone, as late as the 1860s.

The coastguards not only watched for smugglers but also looked out for vessels in danger, though there was still no really organised way to rescue survivors until the Royal National Lifeboat Institution was established. Locally two stations were set up, one at Hayling, the other at West Wittering. The latter was situated on the gravel spit which, until the 1920s, stretched westward from what is today the 'hinge' of East Head.

The Hayling station was established following an incident in January 1865, when a small schooner became stranded whilst attempting to enter Langstone Harbour. Major F.W. Festing,

'Power to enter any Ship, Bottom, Boat....'

The smugglers in Chichester Harbour had one special enemy, the collector of customs revenue. In 1823 William Wilson was commissioned to uphold the law and collect the revenues within the Port of Chichester with

> Power to enter into any Ship, Bottom, Boat, or other Vessel ... and taking with him a Constable, Headborough or other public Officer ... to enter into any House, Shop, Cellar, Warehouse or other Place whatsoever, not only within the said Port, but also within any other Port or Place ... there to make diligent Search, and in case of Resistance, to break open any Door, Trunk, Chest, Case, Pack, Truss or any other Parcel or Package ... for any Goods, Wares or Merchandizes, prohibited to be exported out of, or imported into the said Port, or whereof the Customs or other duties have not been duly paid. And the same to seize to His Majesty's Use, and to put & secure the same in the Warehouse in the Port next to the Place of Seizure ...

West Sussex Record Office, Add. Ms. 2616

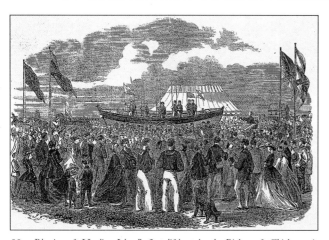

89   *Blessing of Hayling Island's first lifeboat by the Bishop of Chichester in 1865.*

from the Royal Marine Artillery headquarters at Fort Cumberland, organised a rescue boat crewed by local fishermen, and two of the crew were saved. The event was reported in the press and a local lifeboat was demanded. That summer Leaf and Co. of London gave £550 for a lifeboat at Hayling, and the *Olive Leaf* was on station by the autumn. This first boat was replaced by the *Charlie and Adrian* in 1888 and by the *Proctor* in 1914.

By 1924 two new motor lifeboats had been established at Bembridge and Selsey and the Hayling boat was withdrawn. By then, too, the spit on which the West Wittering boathouse stood had been washed away. In addition to the two traditional craft, an Inshore Lifeboat Station has been established within Chichester Harbour on Hayling Island for the benefit of yachtsmen and the few fishermen who still operate out of the harbour and along the adjacent coasts.

Of Mills and Millers

If bread is the staff of life then the story of the miller is the story of civilisation as it has developed over the last several thousand years, for without the miller and his mill the making of bread is a lengthy and time-consuming process. Until the coming of the steam engine which could be used to power a mill, only three types of mill existed. Firstly were the simple water mills which had been introduced into this country before the Norman Conquest; secondly were the windmills which seem to have been introduced by the church sometime in the late 12th century; lastly were the tide mills where the sea was impounded by a wall in which a sluice allowed the millpond to be filled by the rising tide. Although locally at least one such tide mill was in existence in 1086, they were built around here between the late 17th and late 19th centuries.

90 *Sussex mills around the harbour in 1724. This map by Richard Budgen shows watermills (as small paddlewheels) and windmills.*

A steam mill was built at Chichester in 1785, giving an indication of the importance of the milling trade in the harbour area at that time, for by 1800 only 55 such mills had been built in the whole country.

All three types of mill had their weaknesses. Watermills too often stood idle for lack of water in a region where many of the local streams depended on lavants to provide a full flow. Windmills needed a steady breeze; no wind no power, and too much wind and the sweeps could 'run away' causing the mill to catch fire. Often in the case of the earlier post mills the whole structure could blow over in even a moderate gale. A recent authority has stated that tide mills were not extensively built around the coasts of England and Wales, but in the mid-19th century there were some seven or eight in operation around the harbour, a concentration as high as that found anywhere else, due to its tidal nature.

Tide mills were expensive to build but, whilst they could rarely operate for more than eight to ten hours in every tidal day, the power was constant and reliable, even if the miller had to work what today we would call 'unsocial hours', as the tides wait on no man's convenience. The tide mill at Sidlesham was not on the shores of Chichester Harbour, but it was within the Port of Chichester, its owners were Chichester men, and cargoes coming from, and going to, Sidlesham wharf counted as Chichester cargoes. It was Woodrofe Drinkwater who first built this mill in the mid-18th century. He had started life as a mealman and miller at West Ashling; by 1757 he was a merchant of Chichester sufficiently rich to be able to farm the port dues for Chichester Corporation. It was shortly after this that he built the mill at Sidlesham. In 1782 Michael Kingsford, also a merchant of Chichester, bought the mill for £5,500 and improved it further. This was serious money for a man to invest at a time when a labourer was lucky to earn £20 a year, curates were paid £50 and a lieutenant in the Royal Navy on active service received £80. In 1796-1800 it has been calculated that the average value of a windmill in England and Wales was £438, and of a water mill £817. Even in 1816-20 the average value of a steam mill was £3,338. Horsfield, writing in 1835, claimed that Sidlesham mill was one of the largest of its kind in the country, that it could grind a single load of wheat in an hour, and that vessels could come alongside to unload, or lie off waiting for a berth, in perfect safety.

The grain trade made Chichester Harbour important for some three centuries, and it was the mill which made the trade possible. The remains of many of the buildings may still be seen, situated on an arc stretching from Hayling, past Langstone, Warblington and Emsworth and on into Sussex at the Hermitage, through Nutbourne, Broadbridge, Bosham, Fishbourne and Birdham. It has even been suggested that a mill once existed at the head of tidewater on the Lavant at what was once called Apuldram Common.

There is no mention of a mill at Hayling in 1086, which is not surprising as there is no stream there capable of driving even the simplest water wheel, but by 1294 the records of the manor of Hayling Priory show that the monks owned a watermill there worth £3 per year. This must obviously have been some sort of tide mill, probably built at the head of Mill Rythe, though not necessarily at the same place as the 18th-century structure. In 1325 the records show two mills—a watermill worth 13s. 4d. and a windmill worth 6s. 8d.—which probably give a good indication of the relative value of each type of mill. Three sites where windmills once stood have been recorded in Hayling Island. That at North Stoke was in operation as late as the 19th century and may well have been the site of the monks' mill of 1325. We do not know whether the priory's tide mill survived the sequestration of the estate of 1415, but a tide-operated mill stood on Mill Rythe from the mid-18th century. In 1813 this mill was said to have three sets of stones and was associated with a quay capable of taking vessels of 40 tons. In Havant Museum the 19th-century painting of the mill shows a building which appears to be typical of the mid-18th century. In 1875 the lord of the manor decided to rebuild and improve the mill, but before it could become operational again it burned down. Little remains today apart from a small stretch of the quay wall and isolated fragments of the retaining wall of the tidal pond.

The stream which powers Havant's mills flows into Langstone Harbour, although it is likely that some of their produce went through Chichester Harbour. The mills at Langstone, however, are a part of the Chichester Harbour scene. Though new in the mid-18th century, they were certainly not the first mills on the Lymbourne stream which enters the harbour at this point. The Lymbourne flows between Havant and the tithing of Newtimber, otherwise known as the manor of Wade. There was a mill there in 1086 'worth 5s'; when John le Fauconer died in 1305 there was said to be both a wind and a water mill on the manor of Lymbourne. Half a century later when Henry Romyn died, the watermill was said to be worth 'only 20s because it cannot grind in summer due to lack of water'. The present buildings at Langstone are thought to be one of the harbour's main visual attractions and appear in many paintings. The watermill is the older of the two buildings, whilst the millpond may well go back to Domesday, although we cannot be certain of this or that the medieval mills survived the late 14th-century change from arable to pasture. In the early 18th century there was a saltern at the Lymbourne's mouth, and it was not until the salthouse had been pulled down that the watermill was built in the early 1770s. The probable date for the windmill is 1780. At the manorial court in 1786 Thomas Tribe was admitted to the watermill, whilst in the late 18th and early 19th centuries it was the Goodman family who occupied the windmill, both properties being separately owned and managed. Neither survived as working mills into the present century. In 1927 the two were first seen by the artist Flora Twort and, though derelict, they aroused her interest. Between 1932 and 1948 she was the owner and had created the dwelling house we see today. During the last war she offered accommodation to naval officers and scientists stationed locally. One of these was the author Nevil Shute, who under his full name—Nevil Shute Norway—had founded the Airspeed Aircraft Company at Portsmouth in the 1930s. During the war he worked for the Admiralty Scientific Service, some of his ideas coming to him at Langstone Mill.

The mill at Warblington in 1086 stood immediately to the east of the castle and its millpond may still be traced. Mentioned by Longcroft, it is difficult to know when it was abandoned; one would suspect that this occurred early in the 17th century when the park around Warblington Castle was converted to arable, and the inlet to the east of the church shut off from the harbour.

The original mill at Emsworth was the so-called Town Mill, or Lord's Mill, in Queen Street. Dating from at least the 16th century, there may have been one on this site before this, but the earliest reference seems to be in 1570 when Thomas Swyft, miller of Emsworth, died. It may well be the mill referred to by Longcroft belonging to the manor: one wheat mill and one malt mill, both under one roof, let at a rent of £20 in 1632. Towards the end of the 18th century it was leased to Joseph Holloway and John Hendy for the sum of £50 a year. This mill, directly powered by a branch of the Ems, has obviously been rebuilt many times. Mill rebuildings are often necessary because of destruction by fire and 1894 was no exception. The Queen Street mill was totally gutted, only the shell being left. When it was rebuilt in its present form, power was provided by a horizontal water turbine rather than the normal wheel, a much more efficient device and one which was still providing auxiliary power long after the rollers of the mill were powered by electricity.

The Quay Mill at Emsworth seems to have been built in the middle of the 18th century. The pond was so constructed that small vessels could enter at high tide through the single lock

The Langstone Mills: **91** *(top) Decaying in the 1920s;* **92** *(bottom) The conversion, photographed in 1995.*

gate and moor alongside the wall between the mill and the granary. This was a tide mill, although water also came from the Westbrook, allowing a slightly longer run than if the mill was powered solely by impounded tidal water. By the end of the 19th century a steam engine had been added to work the mill when the pond was too low to drive the wheel, and in the 1920s a gas engine was substituted. By about 1930 it ceased to be used as a mill and became a store. Today it is the club house of the Emsworth Slipper Sailing Club.

93 *Quay Mill, Emsworth, in about 1926.*

The Slipper Mill, also a tide mill, was built in the middle of the 18th century by Thomas Hendy, miller and merchant. The mill is actually in Sussex, but it was Emsworth-owned and a part of the Emsworth mill complex of four working mills, two of them tidal. The fourth mill was at Lumley. There was to have been a fifth, as in the late 19th century an additional tide mill was built to the south of the Slipper. Designed to be powered both by the outflow of its tidal pond and also by steam, it seems never to have become fully operational. J.D. Foster used the millpond for many years to season timber and today it serves as the Tarquin Yacht Harbour.

There was a succession of buildings on the Slipper Mill site, mills being notorious for burning down. The last ceased to be powered solely by tidal outflow in about 1940 when power was provided from the National Grid. Production finally ceased in 1966 when the building was sold and converted into houses. The so-called Flour Mill in Queen Street closed in 1970. The building has been converted into offices and workshops. Both mills had ceased flour production long before the final closure. In their last phase—the last mills on the harbourside still working—they were provender mills.

The mill at Lumley dates from the mid-18th century, the great time for the rebuilding of old mills and the building of new ones around the harbour. It was a watermill powered by a leat drawn off from the Ems at Westbourne. During the Napoleonic wars it was leased by Edward Tollervey who had a contract to supply the Admiralty with pork and biscuits. He built bakeries and pigsties adjacent to the mill, using the middlings and any spoilt biscuits to feed the pigs, so reducing costs and increasing profits. It has been said that the end of the war forced him into bankruptcy and that he died a pauper in London, but this does not seem to be the case as he was still living in Westbourne in the early 1820s. The mill worked throughout the 19th century, though latterly the water wheel was assisted by a steam engine. In 1915 it was all but destroyed one night by a fire and was never rebuilt. The mill house, a most interesting building, still survives.

The Domesday mill at Nutbourne is almost certainly not identical with the later tide mill, but situated further up the Ham Brook. One authority has suggested that the tide mill itself dates from the last years of the 17th century and, if that is the case then, apart from the Fishbourne Saltmill, it must be the first of the recent tide mills to have been built. The outline of the millpond may still be traced. Through it runs the trickle of the Ham Brook to pass out into the harbour through a sluice in the wall on which the mill itself once stood. To the south-west, just where the coastal footpath turns sharply towards the north, there may still be seen the remains of the hard where barges used to haul up to load and unload at the mill. In 1845, J. Wyatt, who was then the miller, also called himself a coal merchant, so presumably the pattern there was similar to that of the rest of the harbour: coal in and grain products out. Nutbourne tide mill was still working in 1880, but in 1882 there was a plan to enclose the area between Thorney Island and the Chidham peninsula, the area which today we call the Nutbourne Marshes. The proposal failed, although Stakes Island remains to remind us of the intention, but the plan ended the life of Nutbourne Mill. By 1896 the six-inch Ordnance Survey map marks the 'Old Mill Pond' as 'Mud'.

Cut Mill stood just on the Chidham side of the boundary with Bosham parish; the mill pond lay to the north of the road. It was always a water mill, the pond being supplied in part by a small stream which rises south of Hambrook Common, in part by springs in the bed. In 1832 the miller was J.W. Merrett, but by 1913 the then proprietor was Amos Wakeford who described himself as 'farmer and miller', which suggests that the mill was now only a part-time occupation. Wakeford was still there in the early 1920s, but he does not appear after 1924 and the mill seems to have ceased some time close to that date.

Although eight mills are mentioned in the manor of Bosham at the time of Domesday Book, four of these were in the area which later became the parish of Funtington; one at Old Fishbourne is discussed below, whilst Cut Mill is mentioned above. This leaves just two mills in Bosham to mention, that at Broadbridge and the Quay Mill in Bosham village. Broadbridge Mill was of considerable importance, with a mill pond which stretched to the north of the

94 *Quay Mill, Bosham, in 1902.*

present railway which crosses it by a bridge and embankment. In the Middle Ages it was a corn mill, but in the 15th and 16th centuries there was a fulling mill as well which ceased to exist in the 17th century when the local cloth industry declined. In the latter part of the 19th century the mill was considerably enlarged, adapted to roller milling and given a steam engine, perhaps because the proximity to the railway made the acquisition of fuel more easy. In 1875, when it was still a water mill, the owner was Thomas Gatehouse. By 1882 it is shown as being powered by both water and steam, and by 1903 Thomas Gatehouse and Sons called themselves 'coal and corn merchants' of the Broadbridge Steam Roller Mills. By 1905 Samuel Gatehouse had taken over from his father. According to the local directories the mill was still operational up to about 1915. In 1922 it was partially demolished. Today all traces of the mill buildings have disappeared, although the mill pond remains, and the site is used for housing.

The Quay Mill at Bosham was the manorial mill. The leat is of considerable length and entirely artificial from Broadbridge southwards. Its millpond lies to the north of the church and the various sluices may still be seen. In the early years of the present century the lessee of the mill was Mrs Mary Ann Brown, and the Brown family continued to own the lease until 1955. The mill used water power until the 1930s. By 1934 the trade directory gives the power as being electric, and so it remained as late as 1954. Like the two remaining mills at Emsworth, in the last stages of its operation this was a provender mill, and the grain came and went no longer by barge but by road transport. In 1955 the mill closed, the lease came up for sale and the Bosham Sailing Club was able to negotiate with the Manor of Bosham for their use of the building. They moved in during 1956, and today the mill is their clubhouse.

There were two groups of mills on the harbour. The first was at Emsworth, the second at Fishbourne, but the Emsworth mills had the advantage as far larger vessels could go alongside, whereas at Fishbourne the depth of water restricted traffic to comparatively small barges of less than 40 tons.

In 1086 there were two mills at Fishbourne. These were probably the mills described later as the 'Saltmyll' and presumably tidal, and the 'Freshmyll', no doubt drawing its water from the Fishbourne springs. By 1460 the manorial rental lists three mills: the 'Freshmyll', the 'Lityl Saltmyll' now in 'decay' and a third mill rented to William Nyeman. By 1565 the 'Freshmyll' seems to have disappeared, and by the late 16th century a rebuilt 'Saltmill' seems to have been the only mill at Fishbourne at a time when elsewhere in the harbour mills were in decline. Then early in the 17th century Fishbourne Mill was built. It had a breast shot wheel and, with minor alterations and repairs, seems to have worked more or less satisfactorily until 1917 when it burned down. Its replacement of 1918 still stands, although it was only used as a mill for a very short while, becoming disused about 1928 and derelict by 1944. It spent ten years as a macaroni factory and then in 1958 was converted into flats.

In the 19th century there were three other mills at Fishbourne. The Saltmill, situated on the Bosham side of the creek, was the oldest of the tide mills on the harbour and had been restored in the late 16th or early 17th centuries. In the latter part of the 19th century it was owned by James Shepherd, blacksmith and wheelwright, who put these activities before that of miller, opening his sluices so infrequently that he interfered with the smooth running of Fishbourne Mill itself. Because of this lack of care the mill fell into decay and by 1913, when it came on the market, it was in such a ruinous condition that no-one would buy it.

Because of the problems with the Saltmill the owners of Fishbourne Mill brought a post windmill down to the quay from Rustington in 1857. This had two pairs of stones, could be used to supplement the main mill, but was eventually pulled down in 1898.

95   Salt Mill, Fishbourne, in the late 19th century. The oldest of the harbourside tide mills.

96   Fishbourne's windmill by the water in the 1890s.

The third mill was the so-called Water Corn Mill; also a tide mill, it had been built by John Jeliffe in the 1790s with the aid of borrowed money. It does not seem to have been very profitable as the Farhills, who held the mortgage, took it over, then sold it in 1834. Shortly after this it seems to have been abandoned and today only the foundations remain. The site was well to the south of Fishbourne quay, at the end of what was the embankment of the old tidal mill-pond.

At the foot of Mill Lane just to the east of the one-time mill may be seen Saltmill House where the millers used to live. Part of the present building dates from the 17th century when it was occupied by the Aylwin family. The miller, Nicholas Aylwin, died in 1634; his widow, Eleanor, whose inventory survives, died in 1647. Included in this account of her possessions is the sum of £100, the value of 'The House, orchard, barns, stables and the other appurtenances to the same'. It is unusual for such a document to include real estate and we must be grateful for the insight it gives of the value of such a property towards the end of the Civil War.

In the latter part of the 18th century a windmill was built at Dell Quay, being insured in 1790 for £200. In 1807 and again in 1810 it was described as being able to grind seven loads of wheat in a week, which is slightly less than the mill at Sidlesham could process in a single day. The mill may have been taken down as it does not appear on the 1813 Ordnance Survey map, but a mill did exist in the early 1820s and worked for a further 50 years. By this time the grain trade had begun to leave Chichester Harbour, and cargoes of wheat from the New World had started to arrive in larger ships which preferred to use the ports of Southampton or Liverpool.

The tide mill at Birdham dates from about 1768-70. There is mention of a mill here in 1086, but there is no evidence that it survived until the end of the Middle Ages, nor evidence as to where it stood. In 1767 the dean and chapter of Chichester Cathedral granted ten acres of

97 *Water Corn Mill, Fishbourne, in about 1900. Fishbourne's second tide mill.*

98   *Birdham Mill in about 1931.*

what was mostly marshland in the parish of Birdham to James Ayles of Apuldram, who owned the saltern in the south of the latter parish, and John Reeves, miller of Selsey, in order that they might build a mill. The mill and its tidal pool had been established in their present form by 1770 when the two partners drew up an agreement to divide the building between them. Ayles had the eastern side and built a quay there, and Reeves held the western end. For various reasons the property came into the possession of the Farne family of Court Barn. In 1935 they sold out to Captain and Mrs Caldicott, the mill ceased to work and the mill pond was turned into the first yachting marina on the harbour—one of the earliest in the country—under the name of Birdham Pool. The mill had been water driven until the end, one of the last on the harbour to rely solely on natural energy.

Chichester Harbour was always difficult to enter because of the lack of water over the bar. It became an important trading port in the two and a half centuries which followed the English Civil War, due entirely to the fact that the land around the harbour was so fertile. To take full advantage of their situation local merchants in the 18th century built and rebuilt mills all around the shoreline, but as the pattern of the British trade in grain began to change after 1880, so the commercial use of the harbour declined, the mills became derelict and the small sailing vessels which carried the trade disappeared from the seas and local waters.

XIII

Two World Wars

Each war had a different affect on the harbour and its people. In the Great War the real fighting was mostly in Flanders or at sea. The harbour communities sent their men to war, but were little more involved than other similar communities. During the more recent conflict however, from June 1940 onwards, the harbour was to be increasingly in the front-line, culminating four years later in the invasion of Europe. Moreover, as airpower was now so important, much of the local effort would go on support for control of the skies in addition to the age-old British need to keep control of the seas.

David Rudkin, who as a boy lived in Emsworth between 1914 and 1918, has described what it was like to live there at that time. Already air power was starting to become important. T.O.M. Sopwith had a small factory near Chidham, and some of the plywood components for his aircraft were made at Emsworth in an extension built onto the Queen Street flour mill. Planes constructed locally could be watched as they made their trial flights. In 1917 an airfield was laid out at Southbourne where American pilots were to be trained to fly British heavy bombers to attack Germany. Incomplete at the time of the Armistice, it is thought that no active operations were ever mounted from there.

So far as war-time stringency was concerned, as this was a rural area where many of the families had always been semi self-sufficient, there seems to have been little shortage of basic foods. Fishing within the harbour continued, but the smacks seem to have been either laid up or requisitioned as naval tenders. As many of the younger fishermen were with the Navy, it was the old men and young boys who fished the harbour.

Leisure activities ceased. Before 1914 there had been much activity with regattas and races held from time to time, of which more in the next chapter, but with the war these types of events were no longer staged. George Haines was allowed to keep his yacht moorings at Itchenor, and official permits were granted to those owners who wished to lay up their vessels there for the duration, whilst engaged in the more dangerous occupation of fighting the war.

As the shores of the harbour have been so thinly populated there has always been the fear that spies could easily land and depart as they wished. For this reason Henry VIII's Privy Council acted harshly towards the household and person of Lady Margaret, Countess of Salisbury, in the early 1540s, fearing that messages could go to Rome and priests could steal in. In the mid-18th century the bishop of Winchester, when he found that 'one Morgan, a Popish Priest', had managed to build a Catholic chapel within his Havant estate, complained to the Duke of Newcastle that he feared for the safety of the kingdom as 'illegal correspondence' with the French would be likely to occur.

In both recent wars no one could use the harbour without a permit and the war impinged on the harbour and its inhabitants in many other ways. There were the ever-present wounded to be treated and visited. 'Langstone Towers' and 'Northlands House' at Emsworth both became temporary Red Cross hospitals. Wounded were also to be seen in the streets of Chichester. It says much for the standard of care at the time that so many of those who were wounded eventually recovered. At Chichester, too, there was a prisoner-of-war camp for German soldiers who, under the Geneva Convention, could be given employment. Many could be seen working on local farms.

A number of vessels built in the harbour were also to fall prey to the war at sea. Included in their number was the flat-bottomed brigantine *Fortuna*, built by J.D. Foster in 1892. Of 130 tons, she was originally employed in the coal trade, but when she was sunk by a U-boat off Portland Bill in August 1916 she was owned in the West Country.

The Great War saw the airship at its most important. The British used 'Blimps', non-rigid hydrogen-filled balloons with a simple aircraft fuselage slung beneath. They were used to patrol the Channel and keep a watch for submerged U-boats. The Germans used rigid airships, their gas bags enclosed in a metal framework and the whole covered with canvas. There was a built-in 'bridge', engine nacelles slung outside and, in the later models, accommodation for a crew of some size. One such Zeppelin, the L31, made a bombing raid on Portsmouth in September 1916. It passed over Emsworth on its way home and could clearly be seen caught in a searchlight beam, too high to be damaged by the then rudimentary anti-aircraft defences.

Probably the most serious effect of the First World War on the harbour and its communities may be gained from a study of local war memorials. From largely a rural area with a comparatively small population, too high a proportion of those who had left failed to return. The war ended at 11 a.m. on 11 November 1918. There was to be a short interval of just under 21 years before the next war broke out. Fewer of our countrymen were to die in this conflict but

99   *Bosham War Memorial on Quay Meadow: the unveiling, 11 November 1923.*

on 3 September 1939 no one thought that it would last for so long; indeed no one thought in August 1945 it would end so soon. During its course the people of the harbour were to find themselves heavily involved.

The Second World War divides into three phases: the first lasted from the outbreak until the tragedy and triumph of Dunkirk in 1940; the second phase culminated in the D-Day landings in 1944; the third was the winding-up period from 6 June 1944 until the end of both the campaign in Europe and that in the Far East in 1945. It was during this second period that the contribution of the harbour to the war effort was so important. Firstly, there were the traditions of wooden ship-building and repair, and the yards which existed to carry out these tasks; secondly, there were the holiday facilities which could be adapted as training bases for the crews of the small assault craft if we were to gain a toe-hold on the continent and liberate Europe; thirdly, around the harbour there were a number of airfields from which the RAF could operate defensive missions and launch attacks which weakened German defences and enabled the landings to take place.

In Hayling Island in 1939 there were three holiday camps. In 1940 they were combined to form H.M.S. *Northney*, to became one of a number of landing-craft training bases in the Solent area. In November 1942, following the disaster of the Dieppe raid, when part of the reason for failure seemed to lie in lack of knowledge of the state of the French coast, the Combined Operations Pilotage Parties (COPPS) group was formed. Its base was the Hayling Island Yacht Club, although later volunteers were to be trained in Scotland. At the time of D-Day there were 57 officers and men based there. All members of COPPS had to be proficient canoeists and many were also divers or frogmen. The parties travelled to the beaches where surveys were needed in midget submarines or X-craft. Two of these small craft sailed from H.M.S. *Dolphin* on 2 June to lie off the French beaches and act as markers for the landings. The postponement of the operation meant that their crews had to spend an extra 24 hours in considerable discomfort.

If the crews of the landing-craft were trained in the harbour, then some of the smaller assault craft were actually built there, and in addition the yards carried out repair and maintenance whenever needed. Yards which were particularly active were those at Emsworth, at Mill Rythe on Hayling Island, Combes' yard at Bosham and the Birdham Shipyard. At Bosham and Birdham the equipment supplied by the Admiralty may still be seen. The most productive of all the yards was at Itchenor where quite large craft such as the Fairmile Motor Launches were built, as well as landing craft and other small, fast, vessels. It was in building such craft that the traditional skills of the local shipwrights in the use of timber came into their own.

Another of the lessons learned at Dieppe had been that it was unlikely that an invasion force would be able to capture an undamaged port in sufficient time to use it for the landing and supply of reinforcements. It would be necessary for the invasion force to take its own port with it. This led to the decision to plan for, and construct, the Mulberry Harbours which almost alone made the actual invasion such a success. One of those most closely associated with the early designs was Lieutenant-Commander Robert Lochner, RNVR, who lived at Linchmere in the north-west of Sussex. His widow, Mary, later became a West Sussex County Councillor and a member of the Chichester Harbour Conservancy between 1972 and 1975. None of the vast Phoenix caissons was actually built on the harbour, although four were constructed on Hayling Island near the mouth of Langstone Harbour. One cassion never made it to Normandy and today lies just north of the Hayling Ferry pontoon. The construction firm, Dorman Long, made other Mulberry components on land to the north and east of Burne's yard at Bosham.

In addition to the new airfield at Thorney there were permanent RAF stations at Tangmere and Ford. There were also private airfields at Goodwood, and at Portsmouth, the latter owned

100   D-Day landing craft at Birdham in 1943 or '44. Note the boat turntable on which the craft are cradled in trolleys. The turntable is still in use today.

101   Relics of D-Day landing craft at Itchenor in 1995.

by the Airspeed Company with which Nevil Shute was associated. In Hampshire there was also an RAF training and trials airfield at Gosport, and also the Fleet Air Arm base at Lee-on-Solent. One might have thought that these would be sufficient defences for the Portsmouth area, but they were not, and further airfields had to be established.

In 1940 the harbour was under siege. Strahan Soames was at Emsworth awaiting his call-up that August and remembers vividly the attacks on Portsmouth and on Thorney Island, and the near misses which hit the harbour communities. He witnessed the shooting down of some German aircraft and saw a number on the ground. His diary for the period from 15 August to 21 September records that in Emsworth the siren sounded no fewer than 86 times. Only on five days were there no incidents, whilst on 16 August there were six.

To ward off attacks on Thorney airfield false landing lights were installed across Nutbourne Marshes as a decoy for German bombers. Part of the cabling system still survives. At the beginning of the war another subterfuge at Thorney was camouflage: hedges were painted across the original grass aerodrome to suggest a pattern of small fields from the air.

Not all the planes which came down in Emsworth were German, or were shot down in combat. On 8 February 1944 a Mosquito aircraft piloted by Flight-Lieutenant Arthur Woods crashed in Brook Meadow, after colliding with a Wellington bomber whose crew also perished. In civilian life Arthur Woods had been a film director whose 1930s production *They Drive by Night* is considered to have been one of the classics of that period. The incident is now commemorated by a small plaque on the new bridge over the Ems at the foot of Seagull Lane in Emsworth, in part organised by the Emsworth Maritime and Historical Trust.

In 1943 the decision had been taken that the landings in France would be on the Normandy beaches, and in order to ensure success considerable airpower would need to be deployed. A number of Advanced Landing Grounds were established in West Sussex from 1943, many of which were in the immediate vicinity of the harbour. Advanced Landing Grounds had no permanent buildings, apart from a few corrugated iron hangars open at both ends, in which planes could be serviced and minor repairs carried out. RAF personnel lived mainly in tented accommodation, although nearby houses were occasionally requisitioned. The two most important from the point of view of the harbour were those at Funtington and Apuldram, but others were established at Selsey and Bognor. Built in 1943, most ALGs did not come into constant use until March or April 1944.

By January 1944 it had been agreed that General Eisenhower would be the supreme allied commander, with General Montgomery in command of land forces. Between 19 and 21 April Eisenhower was at the *Ship Hotel* in Chichester to survey the plans. On 26 April the naval staff under Admiral Ramsay moved into Southwick House, near Portsmouth, and by 17 May the landing date had been provisionally fixed for 5 June with the option of the next two days if the weather should be unsuitable. The greater part of the invasion forces was concentrated in Hampshire in two groups: one around Southampton for the western beaches and the American landings, the other around Portsmouth. On the Sussex border, the 3rd British Division was quartered together with some Commandos, Free French troops and Canadians. Stansted House and its grounds was the centre of A2 camp in X sector, A1 was at Rowlands Castle, with the tents hidden in the woods of Havant Thicket, and other camps were at Waterlooville and Crookhorn. This was the force which had been selected to land on Sword Beach, the most easterly of the three in the British/Canadian sector. Before the real invasion a series of trial landings—code-named Exercise Fabius—was to be made. Fabius 2 saw the 50th (Northumbrian) Division, which would lead the assault on Gold Beach, embarked at Southampton and landing in Hayling Bay; Fabius 3 saw the 3rd Canadian Division land on the Wittering beaches,

102 RAF Apuldram. Quickly-erected Blister hangars were built beside the harbour in Quay Field for the Czech-flown Spitfires.

whilst the 3rd British Division, whose targe was Sword Beach, made its rehearsal a Climping, near Littlehampton as Fabius 4.

Because of the weather, the landing were postponed until 6 June. The bombarc ment force which had left the Clyde on 2 Jun reached Land's End by daybreak on the 4th and then turned around and spent the next 2 hours steaming slowly up and down the Bris tol Channel. Some of those embarked in th landing craft spent a most uncomfortable da at anchor off Spithead. No one who was on the beaches at dawn on 6 June will ever forge the sight of the long lines of warships an landing craft. Aboard the old cruise H.M.S. *Frobisher*, lying six miles to the nort of the River Orne, it was possible to see th landing craft closing on the shore and watch the constant stream of aircraft passing overheac H-hour on Sword Beach, the destination of most of those who had started from the area c Chichester Harbour, was 07.25. By 07.30 the first troops were ashore, one of the 3rd Division formations—the 5th Battalion King's Regiment—had embarked at Emsworth, the rest fror near Portsmouth, Shoreham and Newhaven.

Despite the heavy naval bombardment and the gallantry of the military in the landin craft, the whole operation might never have succeeded without the work of the RAF, and i particular that of the pilots flying from the airfields which fringed the harbour. From Thorne Island four squadrons of Typhoon fighters concentrated on ground attacks on German a mour; more Typhoons, this time from Westhampnett, carried out similar tasks against fixe defensive positions. From Apuldram there were three squadrons of Spitfire Mk IX aircra manned by Czech pilots. Providing cover over the beaches to ensure that the Luftwaffe did no interfere with our ground forces, they were to fly more sorties than any other RAF station tha 6 June. Finally there were three squadrons of Mustangs from Funtington engaged in a simila operation. Directing all these attacks was the main RAF operations control room, situated i the hall of Bishop Otter College at Chichester and fully manned from February to Decembe 1944. On D-Day no fewer than 56 squadrons were controlled from there.

D-Day and the landings were not the end of the story of the harbour at war. There was t be a further six-months period when it provided support for the troops in France and, for th RAF at Bishop Otter, six months after that when they directed RAF squadrons operating agains the flying bombs. The end of the war in Europe in May 1945 did not see the immediate end c naval and military activity in the harbour area, although there was some easing of restrictions a to access. Not until August, when Japan capitulated, did any real degree of normality returr but it was only in the spring of 1946 that the people who lived by and on the harbour coul return to their lawful peace-time activities.

XIV

Messing about in Boats

Today the commercial life of the harbour has all but ceased but its waters are far from empty; this is the Age of Leisure and around its shores leisure tends to mean getting out on the water in a boat. Today there are far more hulls afloat locally than there ever were when fishing boats and small coasters sailed to and from the little creeks and ports on the harbour's shores.

The activity described so lovingly by Ratty as 'simply messing about in boats' is not an entirely modern development. From the mid-19th century onwards the leisured classes were taking to the seas and inland waters, whilst encouraging the local fishermen to join them in regattas for which they put up the prizes. It may not be too far-fetched to suggest that it was the children of the local seamen who also learned their future skills by playing with old boats in the years before they joined the family team to help earn the family's income.

If any one man may be given the credit for encouraging the leisured classes of his age to take up the sport of sailing for pleasure, that man is Charles II who, given a small yacht called the *Mary* by the Dutch in 1662, went in for sailing and racing and succeeded in acquiring some 20 vessels before his death in 1685. The yacht fleet ranged in size from small cutters of 25 tons, such as the *Jamie*, to larger vessels, almost small warships, used on government business and as auxiliaries to the fleet. One of the larger vessels was the *Fubbs* of 1683; of 148 tons and ketch-rigged, she owed her name to the fact that Louise de Keroualle, Duchess of Portsmouth, one time mistress of Charles II and mother of the 1st Duke of Richmond of the present creation, had developed a matronly or 'fubbsy' figure. It has been suggested that this yacht was actually stationed at Itchenor under a Captain Darley for the use of the Duchess, said to have been staying locally to keep away from the court. This would appear to be unlikely, given the date of her launch and that Louise was then in good favour at court and remained so until Charles' death in February 1685. Her apartments were in Whitehall, and, according to John Evelyn, rather too elaborate. One assumes she would not leave them so long as Charles was in London. Goodwood House and estate were only acquired by the 1st Duke of Richmond in 1697, so there would seem to be little point in a yacht being stationed in the harbour at any earlier date. Perhaps the nearest that the Duchess came to Chichester Harbour was in September 1683, when the Court was at Winchester for Charles to put in motion his idea of a new royal palace there. Then he came with Louise and other courtiers to Southampton and thence by yacht to Portsmouth with a view to looking at the dockyard. Charles had intended to show Louise over Southsea Castle, but it came on to rain, so the party returned the way they had come.

When Charles died in 1685, James II wished to be rid of his brother's old flames. In August Pepys arranged for the Duchess to go by yacht to Dieppe. She never returned to England, although her son came back in 1692. The *Fubbs* was the last of Charles' yachts to survive in royal service; rebuilt twice, she was finally broken up in 1781, almost a century after her launch.

If a Darley had ever been the captain of the *Fubbs* then it must have been very briefly perhaps in 1684-5, for in 1688 Pepys wrote to Lord Dartmouth, the fleet's commander, pointing out that Captain Sanders, her old commander, was still alive and he had no right to appoint Captain Collins to the post. As it was some 70 years after Charles' death that Darleys appear in the West Itchenor church records, the story cannot be proved.

In the 19th century it became fashionable for those with time to spare to hire a boat from a local fisherman and take a trip on the water. That this could lead to disaster is shown by a tablet in St James' Church, Emsworth, which tells how the Reverend Herbert Morse and three friends were drowned in the harbour when the boat they had hired was overturned by a sudden squall. Unfortunately the sea still takes its toll, and a plaque on the Quay Mill, now occupied by the Emsworth Slipper Sailing Club, records the more recent death by drowning of an Emsworth fisherman.

From the start of the 19th century regattas were held regularly by the various harbour communities. There seem to have been at least two each year, one for the western, the other for the eastern part of the harbour, the latter apparently organised by the Itchenor customs officer who held it there. In the west both Hayling and Emsworth held regattas; official cards for two events organised by Hayling Island have survived in the records at Havant Museum. They were

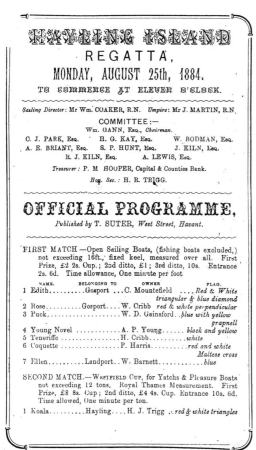

103 *Hayling Island Regatta programme, 1884. Today the Hayling Island Sailing Club is recognised as one of Britain's leading clubs, hosting national and international dinghy racing.*

held on 18 August 1877 and 25 August 1884 and are of considerable interest as they show that both the local fishermen and bargemen were involved, as well as the coastguard, Royal Navy boy seamen under training, and the local amateur yachtsmen. On both occasions there were 11 events and on both occasions the regatta secretary was H.R. Trigg, auctioneer, land agent and surveyor, and author of the *Guide to Hayling Island* of 1892.

In 1877 the first event was listed as being for 'Open Sailing Boats (fishing boats excluded) not exceeding 16 ft.', which would suggest that it was for the amateur sailor. There were seven entries, all apparently of 'gentlemen', three from Hayling, one each from Brighton, Bedhampton, Emsworth and Portsmouth. The second event was for 'Yachts and Pleasure Boats not exceeding 12 tons', all four competitors coming from outside the harbour. There was also an 'Open Barge Match' with entries from Emsworth, Hayling and Portsmouth, rowing races between the various coastguard crews in their four-oared galleys, another for boy seamen in 10- or 12-oared cutters, and one for 'Gentlemen Amateurs'. The tenth event was a race for 'the Committee's Prize' for '*bona fide* Fishing Boats not exceeding 18 feet'; the three contestants all came from Emsworth, the respective skippers being

T. Parham, J. Clark and W. Parham. The regatta held on 25 August 1884 was similar. Once again the fishermen of Emsworth were prominent in the fishermen's race, but this time they were joined by a W. Coombes of Bosham. On this occasion the last race was for amateur swimmers and included George Gatehouse of Chichester and three men from Portsmouth. Once the 1884 activities on the water had ceased, participants and spectators were invited to meet outside the *Royal Hotel* when various land-based events would take place, including an attempt to climb the greasy pole.

Towards the end of the century similar events were held at Langstone, and here in 1901 a trophy was awarded to Ernest Little of the gravel-dredging firm to commemorate his winning races for three consecutive years. The Littles were generous to the people of that hamlet for, whenever there was a national holiday in the summer, they would deck out their barge, the *Gladys*, and set out on a voyage down the harbour with most of their neighbours aboard. By the outbreak of the Great War in 1914 there would appear to have been a number of experienced amateur dinghy rac-

104   Early racing in the harbour. James Parham won the Stansted Challenge Cup presented by George Wilder of Stansted for racing at Emsworth Regatta in 1874. This photograph was taken in 1920 when James was aged 80.

ers and yachtsmen in the harbour. The oyster fishermen, having spent their summers crewing the J-class boats at Cowes, were also very much used to the sort of skills they rarely needed on their winter voyages on the smacks.

Organised yachting, as understood today when the local sailing club is the centre of most harbour activities, seems to have started out of the need for a permanent body to organise the regattas. An Emsworth Boating Club held its first dinner in September 1888, though it may not have had a very long life. A second attempt to found a Sailing Club at Emsworth occurred in 1895 when six Emsworth worthies decided to start one and ordered six boats from the Isle of Wight, all built to the same design. This venture, too, seems to have been short-lived as a correspondent to the *Yachtsman* in 1902 said he had been to Emsworth to see if there was such a club there, had found there was not, and that the principal agent was away in his boat. There were, however, proposals to make a fresh start. That this did probably come about—with the members meeting at the *Ship* public house, holding races and awarding prizes—seems to be borne out by the fact that the Slipper Club possesses a number of trophies which date from the period 1906-14. Those active in this body before 1914 seem to have kept in touch and in 1921 they officially founded the Emsworth Slipper Sailing Club.

The first club on the Sussex side would appear to be that at Bosham, formed in 1907. In 1908 it took over the running of the eastern regatta which was switched to Bosham from Itchenor. Annual events were held until 1914. The first club secretary was the auctioneer, Glyn Martin. In 1920 the club was re-formed as the Bosham and Itchenor Sailing Club and the first post-war regatta was held. However, the men of Itchenor wished to be independent and

105   *Emsworth Regatta in 1905.*

STANSTED PARK, EMSWORTH, SUSSEX,
July 1st, 1919.

DEAR SIR (OR MADAM),

It is proposed to start a Sailing Club in Chichester Harbour with Head-quarters and Club House at Emsworth.

An excellent Club house has been procured, which comprises the old Coast Guard Station and a fair-sized house adjoining; with two good "hards" leading to deep water anchorage. The facilities for small craft sailing in sheltered waters are as good as could be obtained anywhere, and it is hoped ultimately to start a class of small and inexpensive club boats and organize races for them throughout the season. A limited number of bedrooms will be available for Members. A Club boatman would be engaged to look after Members' boats, and take Members to and from the shore.

It is proposed to enrol:

I.   **Life Members** on payment of £25.

These Members would enjoy all the privileges of the Club without payment of any further entrance fee or subscription. These privileges would be extended to one other member of their family. They would have the first call on Club assets in the unlikely event of the Club being wound up (the Club house being the property of the Club).

II.   **Ordinary Members** (ladies and gentlemen) on payment of £2 2s., entrance fee; £1 1s., annual subscription.

III.   **Founder Members** on payment of £5 5s. These members would be entitled to all the privileges of the Club, without further subscription for 5 years.

Ladies will be eligible for membership.

Many promises of support have already been obtained.

Application for membership may be made to any of the undersigned:
CAPTAIN C. J. T. CAVE, *Ditcham Park, Petersfield.*
COMMANDER C. DENISON, D.S.O., R.N., *Aldsworth Farm, Emsworth Sussex.*
MAJOR G. C. WHITAKER, *Stansted Park, Emsworth, Sussex.*

I am, Sir (or Madam),
Yours faithfully,
G. CECIL WHITAKER.

CLUB BOATS.

Six Club Boats of the Sharpie type are now under construction for the Club, and will be ready by Easter. They will be Club property, and there will be races for them at least once a week throughout the season.
The description of the boats is as follows:
L.O.A.—19ft.
Beam—6ft. 6in.
Draught - plate up, 5ins. plate down, 3 feet.
Half decked.
Rig—Leg-of-mutton Mainsail; Roller Foresail

106   *Founding of Emsworth Sailing Club in 1919.*

the 1921 regatta was held there. By 1922 the words 'and Itchenor' had been deleted from the Bosham Club's rule book, and that date is now held to be the official beginning of the Bosham Sailing Club.

At the other end of the harbour, on 21 June 1919, a meeting was held which marks the formal beginning of the Emsworth Sailing Club. By the autumn the club rules had been drawn up, the club burgee was designed and members enrolled. The original subscription was two guineas (£2.10) for entrance and one guinea (£1.05) annually. The club had also bought for £400 what was then called 'The Bathing House', which is the core of the present club house; the name explains why the road beside the mill pond leading to it is called Bath Road. In 1805 Caroline of Brunswick, Princess of Wales, came to stay at Catherington and was expected to come there to bathe in the sea. The *Hampshire Telegraph* of 19 August suggested that she might be going to Emsworth, where it was reported that bathing machines were being built for her use. No one knows whether or not she actually came, but the idea that bathing in either cold, or possibly hot, sea water might be a good thing so impressed the Emsworth grocer Robert Harfield—whose daughter was the wife of John King II—that by 1810 he had built a 'Bath House' at the south-west corner

---

Emsworth Sailing Club

From Trench Dreams to Early Commodores

In the trenches of Flanders the Great War drags on, muddy, bloody and inconclusive into another autumn. But war is more boredom than fighting and during a lull in the shelling two Guards officers fall to yarning about what they will do when it's all over. They are Major G. Cecil Whitaker and Viscount Bury (later the Earl of Albermarle). Listen to Lord Albermarle's own words:

> I happened to say to him how much I enjoyed sailing and then (as one did then) peering covetously into the dim future of where we might find ourselves after the peace was signed—able to resume our avocations—I said to him, "Surely there'll be many young officers of the Brigade who will want to start learning to become helmsmen of small boats but may lack the opportunity to do this? Could one not start a Club in Hampshire or Sussex, what do you think?"... Later ... one day I received a letter from Cecil saying "Our dream has come off for I have secured a house as a Club station and a small fleet of light boats to start with on Emsworth Harbour."

Major G. Cecil Whitaker, who must be singled out as our Founding Father, was never in any sense a 'constitutional' Commodore. He held Flag rank in the Club for most of its first sixteen years, including three terms as Commodore. In 1926 he stood down in favour of the Earl of Bessborough who, living at Stansted may be regarded as 'local'. He was in turn succeeded by his friend, Lt. Cdr. Lord Louis Mountbatten, then living at Adsdean. Lord Mountbatten returned from serving with the Second Destroyer Flotilla to take up an appointment at H.M. Signal School, Portsmouth. When Lord Bessborough invited him to become our Commodore he at first declined, fearing he would not have time to do the job properly. But he was persuaded, and having agreed, did a characteristically thorough job of it until his return to the Fleet ...

Patrick Millen, *The Story of Emsworth Sailing Club* (1979)

---

of the Mill Pond and had advertised it for rent. In the late 19th century the building, still used for its original purpose, was owned by the Cribb family, but by 1895 trade had declined as 'the quality' preferred Brighton shingle to Emsworth ooze. Jack Cribb cut his losses and sold out, and by 1 November 1919 the club had bought it from its then owner, Miss Duffield, for £400. Since then it has been altered and enlarged, but the early 19th-century heart of the building still stands.

The post-1918 period saw the founding of sailing clubs, not just at Emsworth and Bosham, but also at Hayling Island where in autumn 1921 the Hayling Island Sailing Club was formed. The original club house was Quay Cottage on Mengham Rythe, but this was soon replaced by the premises now occupied by the Mengham Rythe Sailing Club. It was not until 1936 that the HISC moved to its present purpose-built home at Sandy Point.

The Dell Quay Sailing Club started in 1925. Its original home was a room in one of the buildings at Dell Quay, but this was badly damaged in the Second World War and its

107   Solent Sunbeam Joy *in the 1930s.* Joy—*number V2—is one of the earliest Solent Sunbeams, built in 1923 and first owned by Geoffrey (later Sir Geoffrey) Knowles, Commodore of Itchenor Sailing Club. Since 1960 she has been owned and raced by the O'Hea family of ISC. Today there are two fleets: Itchenor is the headquarters of the Solent Sunbeams with its sister fleet at Falmouth.*

present home was built in the 1950s. Originally called the Dell Quay Boat Club, its members were as much interested in fishing, or being afloat, as they were in dinghy sailing and racing, but the fishing has ended and the fish suppers for which they were well known are no longer held.

Yachtsmen and dinghy sailors at Itchenor had long felt the need for their own club, and tended to resent the dominance of Bosham on the eastern side of the harbour. Their yacht club came into existence in 1927. Shortly after this they acquired four small 17th-century cottages which were converted to form their club house. The original buildings have been enlarged and improved over the years. During the last war they were requisitioned, first by the Army and then by the Navy, when preparing for the D-Day landings.

By 1932 there were some half a dozen organised sailing clubs in the harbour, but membership, compared with today, was quite small. In that year the Southern Railway published *Yachting on the Sunshine Coast* which, in addition to pointing out how pleasant were the waters of the harbour and how cheap it was to reach the sailing centres from London by its railway lines, gave the approximate memberships of four of the clubs. Thus there were some 100 members at Itchenor, 150 at Bosham, just over 200 at Emsworth and 110 at Hayling. Allowing for slightly smaller numbers for the Slipper and Dell Quay clubs, then the total of all those involved in organised sailing activities might be estimated at about 700; if those outside the clubs are included, perhaps 1,000 enjoyed the waters of the harbour. In 1994 the Conservancy recorded that some 8,050 vessels had paid harbour dues, whilst others launched boats on a weekly or daily basis. Perhaps the number of those 'messing about in boats' on Chichester Harbour today is some 20 times greater than it was 60 years ago.

Because of the number of clubs in the harbour, a regulating body is required to act in arranging inter-club fixtures, seeing that club regattas do not clash, organising the positions of racing marks and channel buoys and generally liaising with whatever local authority has an interest in the water. In March 1924 a Joint Committee of Chichester Harbour Sailing Clubs met at the *Bear Hotel* in Havant. The representatives of the original four clubs present—those of Bosham, Emsworth, Emsworth Slipper and Hayling—stated that its objectives should be: '... to start at the Entrance of the Harbour and to work inwards, mapping out a complete scheme of Buoys and Booms and then to discover ways and means of realising that scheme'.

During the next 15 years the Committee succeeded to a great extent in carrying out its objective. It was to change its name twice. By 1936 it had become The Federation of Chichester Harbour Sailing Clubs. Emsworth Slipper having declined to join, the other three original clubs, those of Bosham, Emsworth and Hayling Island, had been joined in 1929 by Itchenor, and in 1935 by Dell Quay.

At first racing both within and between the clubs was complicated by the fact that the boats were not identical, and it was necessary to organise a system of handicapping whilst attempting to standardise the type of boat owned by the club members. At first these standard classes were basically *Chichester One Designs* but by 1939 it had been decided that a 'National' class should be adopted, and the *12ft. Design* was chosen. In 1937 it had been proposed to build a *Chichester Harbour 18 ft. Restricted Class*. The first was designed by Colonel Burne; the last of the seven constructed was built by David Bowker at Burne's yard in the 1960s but the class was superseded by the *18 ft. Nationals*.

The war brought all sailing in the harbour to a standstill. The yacht club buildings were requisitioned and not handed back until early 1946, but once hostilities were over a number of new clubs were formed and joined the Federation. The first of these was the Langstone Sailing Club; in October 1945 a meeting was held at the *Ship Inn*, Langstone, the decision to form a club was carried, and an arrangement was made with the licensee to use the old malting loft to the rear of the premises. By 1946 the club was formed and had applied to join the Federation.

Two other clubs joined in 1946. The first was Emsworth Slipper Club, one of the oldest on the harbour, the other a new venture. The RAF had been at Thorney Island since 1939, and had flown and fought from there during the war years. Now peace had come and there was time to settle down and enjoy the area. The RAF station adjoined the harbour, so nothing was easier than to establish the Thorney Island Sailing Club as an important base for the Royal Air Force Sailing Association. The RAF has since left Thorney but still maintains its interest in the club. Today, under Army occupation, there is the addition of its Water Sports Centre.

One of the members of the new Langstone Club was S.Z. (Sinbad) Milledge, a scientist and mathematician who developed the *Portsmouth Yardstick and Langstone Tables* to improve the system of handicaps in races where the entries were made up of many different types of craft. These tables were eventually taken over and used throughout the Federation and elsewhere. Though now overtaken by the use of computer calculations, *Portsmouth Yardstick* numbers still provide a national handicapping system. This 'appliance of science' was a great improvement on the somewhat arbitrary rules of the 1877 Hayling Regatta, when, for open sailing boats, there was to be 'a time allowance of one minute per foot' with 'one minute per ton' substituted for the larger vessels.

Not all the boats in the harbour were racing dinghies; many were larger, and often the owners were more interested in cruising. In 1948 the Federation established its Cruising Committee for this section of the sailing fraternity and, after various changes of name and status, this had become by 1971 the Chichester Cruiser Racing Club, as it is today. In 1950 some

The International 14

108   *The Itchenor Gallon. Stewart Morris (centre) receives the solid silver gallon tankard from Itchenor Sailing Club Commodore, T.D. McMeekin, in 1936 for* International 14-foot *dinghy racing. This trophy is second only to the Prince of Wales' Cup, the premier prize for this class of racing. Famous names such as Peter Scott, Uffa Fox and Stewart Morris have been heavily involved in the development of* International 14 *racing.*

109   *Chichester Harbour helmsmen. Stewart Morris (left) an Michael Peacock, two of Britain's most notable dinghy helmsmen have raced regularly with Itchenor Sailing Club. They are shown her at Falmouth in 1966 after Michael won the prestigious Prince o Wales' Cup for* International 14 *racing, which he won five time in all. Stewart finished second on this occasion, and in all won the cu twelve times.*

110   *Harbour racing. Michael Bond (left) and Michael Peacock of Itchenor Sailing Club with* Harrier. *Chichester Harbour's sheltered waters are ideal for dinghy racing and Itchenor Sailing Club has always been the first home in the harbour for the* International 14.

residents of West Wittering decided to form their own club with its club house at Snow Hill Creek. By 1952 it had joined the Federation and today is unique in the harbour in insisting that only West Wittering residents may join. Also in 1950 the Federation became an affiliated member of the Royal Yachting Association and the Mengham Rythe Sailing Club was founded, joining the Federation almost immediately. The club house of this new arrival was that which the HISC had left in 1936. As in the case of the Dell Quay Club, many of the original members were as interested in fishing as in sailing, but here too the fishing and the fish suppers have ceased.

Hayling Island: Home of Sailboarding

Most of us associate the sport of sailboarding with the west coast of the United States, but it all actually started here in Hayling Island.

During the summer of 1958 Peter Chilvers, then a schoolboy of 12, began experimenting with a piece of plywood, a tent flysheet, some curtain rings and an old wooden pole. The results were spectacular and the rest, as they say, is history.

Peter eventually went into full-time production of sailboards and even managed to successfully sue the American Windsurfing International over patent infringements.

Havant Museum

11   Messing around on ice. The Shaw family go sightseeing around the ice-bound schooner Kathleen and May *off Bosham Hoe during the big freeze in 1962-3. Built in 1900 she worked as a collier and is now preserved by the Maritime Trust at Southwark.*

Arthur Ransome in the Harbour

Author and journalist Arthur Ransome is best remembered today for his twelve classic children's adventure books which began with *Swallows and Amazons* in 1930. Ransome was essentially a countryman and the books reflect his own enjoyment of open air pursuits, his concern for conservation and his passion for sailing small boats.

Ransome first sailed into Chichester Harbour in March 1952 aboard his new 6-ton centre-cockpit sloop, *Lottie Blossom*. At this time he was living in London and had just collected the boat from David Hillyard's boatyard in Littlehampton. There was hardly wind to fill his new red sails as he left with Evgenia, his Russian-born wife, at half-past five in the morning. He moored at Itchenor just before ten o'clock, having motored all the way. Ransome kept a detailed log, and he carefully noted that the harbour dues were 8 shillings (40p) a month and that a mooring cost 16 shillings (80p).

A month later they moved *Lottie Blossom* into Birdham Pool, the only marina in the harbour in those days. The log records: 'Cast off moorings 10 a.m. Stuck on the mud just outside Birdham Lock ... The RCC chart shows a generous sweep round in to the lock, whereas in fact one should hug the shore on the starboard hand ... Berth 10/- [50p] a week ... Had a good look when the banks uncovered, & shall not make that mistake again.'

They soon began to find their way around the harbour: '10.45 cast off mooring and just after low water explored Bosham Creek, which we had never seen ... Went up fairly near to Bosham, to the last of the things that looked as if they might draw 4 feet, and then went down again ... beat up the Emsworth channel. Anchored for lunch 1 p.m. Sailed at 2.45 ... under sail only, with variable wind, up through Itchenor ... We had a grand day.' At Bosham they found the ketch *Peter Duck*, which Ransome had once owned, and on another visit they picked up a mooring and rowed to the hard by the old mill. Here they fell into conversation with a man who showed them another of his previously-owned boats, the *Racundra*, in which, thirty years earlier, Ransome had crossed the Baltic from Riga to Helsinki. Ransome's account of that voyage, *Racundra's First Cruise*, has become one of the best-loved of all cruising yarns.

The following May they returned with a new *Lottie Blossom*: a similar Hillyard, but with an aft cockpit. Ransome's log tells the story of how he caught eels, watched the birds and saw porpoises off the harbour mouth. They made a point of stocking up at the Lock Stores at Birdham, and on one occasion bought two dozen jars of honey from Stanley's Farm. Sometimes they used a friend's mooring off Mengham Rithe and were entertained by the sight of other boat users capsizing and running aground. Even in those days the

There had been a yacht club at Birdham since at least the end of the last war; indeed it may even have started when Birdham Pool was first converted into a marina in the 1930s. Unlike the other clubs in the harbour, it was not owned by its members but was a proprietary club. The sailing section of the Birdham Yacht Club was admitted to the Federation in 1952 but, after nearly 40 years of membership in 1991, it ceased to exist.

When the old salterns were converted into Chichester Yacht Basin there was scope for a new club for those yachtsmen who kept their craft in the marina. Chichester Yacht Club was founded in March 1967; its burgee and initials were the same as those of the old Chichester Yacht Company which had existed in the 1930s to serve the interests of a number of owners of

112/113   Arthur Ransome (inset) with his boat Lottie Blossom *at Birdham in 1953.*

harbour was busy and Ransome noted that he needed the engine to 'dodge a million Fireflys, [International] Fourteens, Flying Fifteens and what not who were racing.' The Ransomes cruised to the Beaulieu River, Yarmouth and Cherbourg, and with Ransome now aged 70, they returned for their final season afloat in 1954.

Having agreed that their sailing days were over, the Ransomes brought *Lottie* to Itchenor one last time. During a desperate scramble to pick up a mooring after the engine had failed, they both badly damaged a hand and feared they would be unable to return the boat to Littlehampton. However, the help they needed was quickly found: 'The very nice chap who supplies water and oil from the float said "Borrow mine," and held up two very capable paws, and I did so.'

Roger Wardale

speed boats who kept their craft at the Salterns end of the Chichester Canal. Their club house on the canal side was called the *Egremont*, after the original inn built there by the canal company in the 1820s. Chichester Yacht Club celebrated its Silver Jubilee in 1992 by building a new club house on the edge of the harbour next to the old canal lock.

In 1964 the Federation not only changed its name to that which it bears today, but it also altered its constitution to admit the sailing schools, yards and other bodies with an interest in the maritime use of the harbour. In 1968 the Emsworth Cruising Association, founded in 1965, also joined, as did the Prinsted Boat Club, although the latter unfortunately failed to survive for more than a few years.

114   Chichester Yacht Basin in 1972. To the left of the main service road is the harbour end of the disused Portsmouth-Arundel Canal. Still in water it is home to a string of houseboats. Top left is Birdham Pool, one of the first marinas in the country, dating from 1937. Chichester Yacht Basin first opened in 1964.

In the 1960s the Federation was increasingly worried by the fact that there was no real unity in the harbour. The Hampshire side was under the control of the Havant and Waterloo UDC, and the Sussex side was the preserve of the City of Chichester; there were two Harbour Masters, two sets of rules and bylaws, two speed limits and two quite different traditions. In Sussex the City of Chichester appointed sailing nominees to its Harbour Committee; at first they were nominated by the individual clubs but by 1963 they were chosen by the Federation. In 1968 Chichester set up an Advisory Committee to which the Federation was able to send four members. In Hampshire the Havant and Waterloo UDC had nothing similar until its own Advisory Committee was established in spring 1969 and on which were five members appointed by the Federation. Already there were moves afoot to unify the harbour, and it was pressure from the Federation amongst others which led to the establishment of the Chichester Harbour Conservancy in 1971.

In 1994, of the 8,000 or so vessels in the harbour, those in the 3-5.2m category—which basically comprised the dinghy fleet—accounted for about half this number. In 1976, five years after the Conservancy came into being, the proportion was 57 per cent; in 1994, 50° per cent. During the same period the percentage of vessels over 8.5m has increased from 12 per cent to 17 per cent and, although the numbers are still small, an increasing number of these are motor cruisers. If the size of the fleet may be measured by the number of swinging moorings and marina berths, then in 1974 there were 2,588 of the former and 1,470 of the latter; by 1990 these had increased to 3,036 and 1,983 respectively. The number of leisure craft in the Solent area is also increasing; by 1985 there were some 30,000, of which some 8,000 were in Chichester Harbour compared with 3,471 in the Hamble and 2,340 at Lymington.

Amongst changes which have helped to conserve the visual aspect of the harbour and to save important buildings for posterity, mention must be made of the rescue of the Quay Mill at Bosham. When this finally ceased to fulfil its original function the Bosham Sailing Club bought it and converted it into its club house, replacing the old motor torpedo boat which had lain alongside the Raptackle and served as the club house since the end of the war. The second mill conversion was at Emsworth where the once tidal Quay Mill was taken over by the Slipper Sailing Club in 1977. The conversion of this building earned the club awards both from the Civic Trust and the Solent Protection Society. The clubs encourage the young to sail and to care for their environment. They are a vital part of the life of the harbour and long may they flourish.

115/116   Slipper Sailing Club, Emsworth. The converted Quay Mill is now the clubhouse. Inset: Solent Protection Society award for the conversion.

Yachting traffic statistics for the harbour during the past 30 years have indicated only a marginal increase in the numbers of boats afloat. At peak summer and holiday weekends there may be congestion at certain pinch points, but at other times only a few yachts will be sailing, so that the harbour is left to the birds. Each club has its annual programme of dinghy racing from April to October, with some hardy souls continuing to race throughout the year. The clubs between them host ten regattas and about 60 other events including national and international championships, but racing is only a part of the picture as the majority of sailors prefer just to cruise the harbour, enjoying its scenery and 'just messing about in boats'.

117   *Reflections: Chairman of Chichester Harbour Conservancy, David Jones, aboard* Mary Ransome, *his Peter Duck class ketch based on a design by Laurent Giles for Arthur Ransome of* Swallows and Amazons *fame. Ransome cruised the harbour in the early '50s.*

Chichester Harbour Conservancy

In the years immediately after the last war the existing harbour authorities became increasingly inadequate at coping with the pressures from the recreational use of Chichester Harbour. So long as the use of the harbour had been confined to locally-based fishing craft and a handful of small coasting vessels the authorities could manage, but by the 1960s they were faced not simply with a great increase in the numbers of vessels in the two harbours, but also with the fact that there was increasing recognition of the landscape and ecological importance of the area and the need for land and water to be managed in an integrated way.

To understand the basic problem it is first necessary to examine the historical development of the management of the harbour from the late 17th century until the 1960s.

By 1680 the government of Charles II had made the western limit of the Port of Chichester the boundary between the counties of Sussex and Hampshire, thus dividing the harbour which before that date had been treated for customs purposes as a single whole. At the same time the right of the City of Chichester to control the Port of Chichester, to charge dues and to insist that Dell Quay would be the only place of landing, was granted. This left the Hampshire part of the harbour within the Port of Portsmouth for customs purposes, but ensured that as far as trade was concerned the merchants and fishermen of Emsworth were not liable to any dues other than those which individual merchants charged each other. There was to be no harbour authority as such on the Hampshire side for over 200 years.

From the early 19th century the buoyage and pilotage in the western part of the harbour was entirely in the hands of the local fishermen, according to Walter Butler writing in 1817, the oldest of whom 'has the care of boomage or fixing booms to denote the channel, for which he receives 1s. annually from each vessel belonging to the port...'. There is little evidence to show that this system was not continued for Emsworth until the last years of the century, for the vestry of the parish of Warblington had no powers at all over the harbour. Then in 1894 the parish became the Warblington Urban District, and in 1896 an Act of Parliament gave the new authority the right to manage Emsworth Harbour. This was defined as being

> all that area below high water mark in or bordering on the Counties of South-ampton and Sussex lying between Hayling Island, West Thorney and the mainland and defined by an imaginary line drawn from Longmere Point in West Thorney to Black Point on Hayling Island and an imaginary line drawn from the point where Hayling Bridge joins Hayling Island aforesaid to the point on the shore of the mainland in or near Langstone where the Parishes of Havant and Warblington meet ...

This allowed the UDC to set and collect tolls and to borrow money for the improvement of the harbour, but it also declared that the ancient rights of Chichester and the lords of the local manors were not to be challenged.

Chichester Corporation had always been careful not to become too closely involved in the administration of the harbour on the Sussex side, no part of which lay within its area, preferring to lease the tolls at Dell Quay to a local businessman. He would collect what was due and use a part of this to provide such simple navigational aids as served the needs of the local fishermen and coastal traders using the harbour. As the principal traffic during the 18th and 19th centuries was coal coming in and grain going out, it became the custom for the lessee to be a dealer in these commodities. The last of the line of Chichester merchants leasing the harbour was the firm of J. Sadler, millers and dealers in coal and grain. When they failed to renew their lease in 1937, as water traffic had all but ended, Chichester applied to Parliament for its own Act, the Chichester Corporation Act of 1938, which granted new powers in relation to the harbour. A Harbour Sub-Committee was established, an official Harbour Master was appointed to replace the unofficial George Haines, and three members of the sailing community were co-opted to serve on, and advise, this new harbour authority. On the Hampshire side, the recently-formed Havant and Waterloo UDC took over the running of the Emsworth part of the harbour in 1932. They too appointed a Harbour Master and later, well after the war, set up an unofficial advisory committee drawn from local harbour users. In 1968, the advisory committee was made official and, in the same year, the Chichester Harbour Advisory Committee was set up by the City Corporation, and four Federation members were appointed. Thus, both local authorities had made considerable efforts to ensure that harbour users were well represented in decision-making, a precedent followed when the Conservancy was created a year or two later.

118 *Vice-Admiral Sir Geoffrey Thistleton-Smith, Chairman, 1971-5. That the Conservancy was so successful in bringing together such a wide range of harbour interests owes much to his central role in creating a fund of goodwill and understanding in its early years.*

Nationally, the early 1960s saw an increasing interest in the environment: National Parks were being established and there was even a suggestion that the harbour area might become the first National Water Park. In the event, the land surrounding Chichester Harbour was declared to be an Area of Outstanding Natural Beauty (AONB) in 1964. Two years later, partly at the prompting of the Federation, partly by other pressure groups, the counties of Hampshire and West Sussex set up a working party to review the future of the harbour and its hinterland. *The Chichester Harbour Study*, which was mainly the work of John Jefferson, the West Sussex County Planning Officer, took two years to complete; in its presentation in 1968, the basic message was that the two harbour areas ought to be combined and administered by one authority and that this authority should also be responsible for the AONB as 'development on the water is bound up with development on the land'.

A steering group was formed on which sat representatives of both County Councils,

> ### '... an integrated whole ...'
>
> Although the harbour and its surroundings mean different things to different people, the recreational and commercial value of the area cannot be separated from its environmental and landscape value. The harbour is not a series of segments: it is an integrated whole of landscape and physical features. The geographical characteristics of the area provide excellent sheltered facilities for sailing. But in turn, the large inter-tidal area which is a feature of that geography is home for the many species of plants, birds and fish which in turn provide the attraction to those who wish to observe or harvest wild creatures. Sailing itself is a major feature of the landscape and undoubtedly is one of the factors which attract visitors to the area. All of these interests are inter-linked and those who follow them share a common purpose in the protection and well-being of the harbour and its surroundings.
>
> For this reason, there should never be any dispute over the aims of the Conservancy, only its priorities.
>
> *Managing Chichester Harbour* (1993)

together with others from Chichester City and Rural District Councils, Havant and Waterloo UDC, the Chichester Harbour Federation and one member representing the Nature Conservancy and the Countryside Commission. This steering committee was serviced by West Sussex County Council officers. The chairman was Vice-Admiral Sir Geoffrey Thistleton-Smith— later to be the first chairman of the Conservancy. The leading member from Hampshire was

David Pumfrett, later Conservancy vice-chairman, and its second chairman. This committee was responsible for drawing up the main provisions of the Chichester Harbour Bill, which was presented to Parliament in 1970 and became law in August 1971.

A leading role in all this was taken by Geoffrey Godber, Clerk to West Sussex County Council, and himself a keen sailor. With David Durbin as his deputy, he managed the complicated negotiations which resulted in the Bill's successful passage. One important area on which compromises had to be made concerned the role of the Conservancy in the town and country planning process. It had originally been proposed that the Conservancy would be the planning authority for the harbour area, but this was dropped in the light of objections from the local authorities who agreed instead to recognise the Conservancy as the official joint advisory committee for the AONB and to consult it on relevant planning policies and development proposals. This arrangement has proved most effective.

119 Geoffrey Godber, Clerk, 1971-5. With the wisdom of a lawyer, a lifelong interest in boating and a deep love of the countryside, Geoffrey Godber brought a rare combination of expertise to the difficult job of engineering the legal basis of the Conservancy.

Another area of discussion concerned membership of the Conservancy and, in particular, the arrangements for the representation of the views of harbour users. Some—such as the RYA and the Emsworth Fishermen's Federation—sought direct representation on the Conservancy, but eventually settled for membership of the statutory Advisory Committee established by the 1971 Act. This drew on the successful experience of the former harbour authorities in consulting harbour users and, crucially, provided a central role for the Advisory Committee, on which a wide range of interests is represented, in the Conservancy's decision-making processes. It is to the wisdom of these provisions in the 1971 Act that much of the considerable success of the Conservancy in balancing competing interests is attributed by informed observers. (For a list of the membership of the Advisory Committee see Appendix 2.)

The Act provided that there should be a majority of County Council members on the Conservancy as the body was entitled under the Act to precept on the counties for funds to maintain and improve the Amenity Area 'for the occupation of leisure and recreation and the conservation of nature'. This Amenity Area must not be confused with the AONB. In Hampshire, the two largely coincide, but in West Sussex there are areas of the AONB outside the Amenity Area. The Act laid two principal duties on the Conservancy: care of the Amenity Area was the second; the first was to maintain and improve the harbour 'for the use of pleasure craft and such other vessels as may seek to use the same'. (For the various boundaries of the harbour, the Amenity Area and the AONB see Appendix 5.)

Transfer

Under the provisions of the Chichester Harbour Conservancy Act, 1971 the Conservancy came into being on the 1st October of that year, and the Clerk and Treasurer of the West Sussex County Council were appointed Clerk and Treasurer of the Conservancy respectively. The harbour undertakings of Chichester City Council and Havant and Waterloo Urban District Council were transferred to the Conservancy on the 1st January, 1972 by which time all the necessary preparatory work had been completed, and with the co-operation of the previous harbour authorities the transfer was accomplished smoothly and efficiently.

The full-time harbour staff of the previous authorities were transferred to the Conservancy in accordance with the Act, and an interim organisation adopted whereby the Harbourmaster's office at Itchenor became the main harbour office and arrangements were made for the continued use of accommodation at Emsworth in the Depot in North Street owned by Havant and Waterloo Urban District Council until satisfactory alternative arrangements could be made. Lt. Cdr. Hard, the Harbourmaster for the Chichester City Council, was appointed Harbourmaster of the combined Chichester and Emsworth Harbours, and Lt. Cdr. Thompson, previously Harbourmaster for Havant and Waterloo Urban District Council, was appointed his Deputy. Consideration of a long-term organisational plan has been deferred until the Conservancy's policies relating to the administration of the harbour and the exercise of their functions in the amenity area have been established, and in the meantime every effort is being made to ensure the efficiency of the harbour management.

Chichester Harbour Conservancy First Annual Report, 1972

The first meeting of the Conservancy was held on 21 October 1971: Trafalgar Day. Appropriately, the chairman of the steering committee, Vice-Admiral Sir Geoffrey Thistleton-Smith, was elected first Chairman of the Conservancy. Sir Geoffrey's contribution to Chichester Harbour cannot be overstated and it is a particularly happy circumstance that sees his son-in-law, Lieutenant-Colonel David Jones, as Chairman of the Conservancy during its Jubilee Year. At the first meeting, Geoffrey Godber was appointed Clerk to the Conservancy and David Durbin served as Deputy Clerk. The County Treasurer of West Sussex was appointed Treasurer to the Conservancy. Michael Holdsworth, County Secretary for West Sussex County Council, became Clerk on Godber's retirement in 1975 and has served in that office for over 20 years, with John Godfrey as his deputy.

During the first six months of 1972, the Conservancy members and officers were en-=gaged in the task of uniting two disparate organisations which involved instituting a single level of harbour dues, examining the mooring charges in the two harbours and bringing them in line, and seeing how the Conservancy could fulfil its function of maintaining and improving the Amenity Area. At first, the members tried to do all the work themselves. Five working parties were established to deal with the subjects of Finance, Amenity, Management, Moorings and Navigation, members of both the Conservancy and the Advisory Committee being involved. During this period, the Chairman spent much of his time on simply running the harbour, which is not what the role of a Chairman ought to be, so in the latter half of 1973 a study was made by West Sussex County Council officers on the question of 'The Future Administrative Structure of the Conservancy'.

120   *The Conservancy in session, November 1995. The Chairman, Lieutenant-Colonel David Jones, is flanked by three principal officers: (on his left) Captain John Whitney, Manager and Harbour Master, and (next but one) Helen Kilpatrick, Treasurer, and (on his right) John Godfrey, Deputy Clerk. Author John Reger—representing Hampshire County Council—sits at the centre table near John Godfrey.*

121 *Lieutenant-Commander Freddie Hard. The Conservancy's first Harbour Master, 1971-4.*

122 *Captain Ian Mackay. The Conservancy's second Harbour Master, 1974-88.*

123 *(left)   Chichester Bar Beacon. The seawards approach to the harbour mouth was made much safer by Harbour Master Captain Ian Mackay in the '70s. The old navigation light was too low and often confused against the background of Hayling Island street lights. After hours at sea on a cold and very dark January night the Harbour Master's personal survey led to the light being more than doubled both in height and power. A morse system was added to transmit information about wind strength and direction, and the beacon was one of the first in the country to provide radio directional finding for recreational craft in poor visibility. Power was generated by a solar panel. This equipment was removed from the beacon in 1993, superseded by satellite navigation.*

124 *(right)   Office saga. The Harbour Office at Itchenor now occupies 'Ferryside', shown here in 1963 when it was still a private house. At this time the Harbour Master, his staff and workshop were cramped into a converted ship's lifeboat moored on the Hard. The Harbour Master's secretary, Ann Fox, remembers how sea-sick she felt at her desk during high tides and stormy weather and on more than one occasion she had to abandon ship! The harbour authority, Chichester City Council, decided to solve the problem by building brand new accommodation right on the Hard, shown here in course of erection. There was uproar in the village - and beyond - at the insensitivity of the City Council in interfering with the free use of the Hard and ruining the view across the water to Bosham and the Downs. They were forced to back down and demolished the building. Eventually 'Ferryside' was purchased for the City Council's Harbour Office which was soon to be transferred to the new Harbour Conservancy in 1971.*

As a result, it was decided to appoint a Manager/Harbour Master who would be the Conservancy's principal officer, caring both for Chichester Harbour *and* its Amenity Area. The post was advertised in February, the requirement being for 'an experienced practical seaman, with knowledge of navigation marks, moorings, etc. and capable of handling small boats and yachts'. Amongst those applying was Captain I.S.S. Mackay, FRIN, RN, who was duly appointed to the post in April 1974. He took over from the Conservancy's first Harbour Master, Lieutenant-Commander Freddie Hard, RN, who had served in this post since 1957. Captain Mackay was to remain in charge for the next 14 years, and his imprint lies upon it still.

The assets inherited by the Conservancy in January 1972 were not very substantial considering the size of the harbour and the work that was needed to be done. They comprised Dell Quay itself and the buildings upon it, some of which were leased to other parties, and the Harbour Office at Itchenor, called 'Ferryside', which was shared with the Customs Office and the Marine Section of the Sussex Police. 'Ferryside' itself was so called because it had for very many years been owned first by the Rogers family, and then by the Haines, who had run the Bosham Ferry for so long that no one could remember when they had started.

By the 1960s it was no longer needed by its owners, whilst there was a great need for a Harbour Office at Itchenor. The building was bought by West Sussex County Council and leased to Chichester Corporation to become the Harbour Office. Since 1972 both the police and the customs authorities have moved out and the Conservancy has expanded to fill the whole building.

In addition to these structures, and one or two buildings leased as stores, the Conservancy inherited a small number of water craft and, most important of all, three leases of mudland

125 *The Conservancy's new patrol boat,* Aella. *Joan Pusinelli names the boat in 1990. On her immediate right are Captain John Whitney, the Harbour Master, and Nigel Pusinelli, Chairman of the Conservancy.*

on which had been laid moorings set down by the previous harbour authorities. Two of the leases were from the Crown Estate Commissioners because normally all land below low water mark is held to be Crown property. One such lease covered a part of the Emsworth Channel, the other applied to Crown mudland in West Sussex. The third concerned the mudlands claimed by the Manor of Bosham, probably due to its having once been royal demesne and guaranteed to that manor by both the Chichester Corporation Act of 1938 and the Conservancy's Act of 1971. All in all, when it took over the harbour in 1971, the Conservancy found that it owned some 600 moorings in the Emsworth and Itchenor Channels.

The question of moorings agitated the yachtsmen for some considerable time, for the policy of both the old authorities had been to lay more and more moorings in order to increase their revenues. As a result, both of these policies and the habits of years, when moorings had been laid on private land as the owner thought fit, the fairways were becoming too crowded for safety. The Conservancy agreed that there should be a complete rearrangement of moorings in all the channels to enable the fairways to be widened. Within the harbour, the Conservancy recognises three classes of moorings: there are those laid by the Conservancy on its own land; those laid by boatyards and other individuals on land owned or controlled by the Conservancy under a rental agreement; moorings on privately-owned land licenced by the Conservancy. In 1994 there was a total of 552 Conservancy-maintained moorings out of a total of 5,019 moorings throughout the harbour.

One of the more recent problems facing all harbour authorities and clubs who lease Crown mudland is that the Crown Estate Commissioners have a duty to maximise their revenues. When leases fall in new rentals are far higher than they were in the past and the mooring holder

26 Joan Edom. Responsible for Nutbourne Marshes, the Conservancy's first nature reserve, Joan was the first Nature Conservation Warden in the harbour. Working tirelessly in the interests of conservation in a completely unpaid and voluntary capacity, she had considerable influence in laying the foundations of the Conservancy's work in this field.

finds he has to pay a higher licence fee. Apart from the licence fees, the Conservancy has two other sources of revenue, other than the precept on the two County Councils. One is the money raised by harbour dues, used to maintain the navigational aids in the harbour and paid by every boat according to its size, and the other comes from the mooring charges which are used to maintain the moorings themselves. Together, these two sources of income are used to finance the harbour authority side of the Conservancy's work.

As mentioned previously, the Conservancy may precept on the two County Councils to an amount determined by the Act. So far this maximum has never been demanded. It is the Conservancy's policy that this money should be used to improve the environment of the harbour. One way of improving the local environment is for the Conservancy to purchase areas of land or mudland which need to be taken into care'. The first so treated was the area called the Nutbourne Marshes. This was bought in 1976 and is now a designated Local Nature Reserve, wardened by the Conservancy. More recently the Conservancy leased Eames Farm on Thorney Island from West Sussex County Council.

The harbour is an important wintering area for large numbers of waders and wildfowl, one of the most important species being the Brent Geese which appear in November and go north in the spring to their breeding grounds near the Arctic Circle. Surveys of wintering wader and wildfowl have been carried out almost from the start by the Conservancy's voluntary wardens. In 1981 the first Amenity Officer was appointed to advise the Conservancy how best to use the limited resources available for that area.

In 1982 the harbour was re-notified as a Site of Special Scientific Interest (SSSI). Then in 1986 it was designated a Ramsar Site, giving the harbour international recognition as an outstanding wetland site. In 1987 a Conservation Warden was appointed.

When the Conservancy took over the harbour there was adequate provision for waterborne activities, with numerous, well-organised sailing clubs, but very little provision for land-based activities, yet the Conservancy had been set up to support all the forms of leisure which could be enjoyed in the harbour and the Amenity Area. Providing such a balance has been difficult, but progress has been made. The old ferry to Bosham had ceased to run before the

127 Anne de Potier, the Conservancy's Conservation Warden. When Joan Edom retired from her honorary position in 1987 Anne took over in the following year as a full-time member of staff with a much wider brief to warden the entire 22 square miles of the harbour. The role includes data gathering, habitat management and wildlife conservation.

128   Opening of Emsworth jetty in June 1995 by Lieutenant-Colonel David Jones, Chairman of the Conservancy.

129   Too many cars ... The approach to Chichester Harbour and the Manhood, summer 1995. These coastal and harbour shores are a honeypot for weekend visitors.

Conservancy was established. In 1976 it was restarted on a summer-only basis and the operation still continues. In 1984 the water bus tours were begun. Sponsored at first, they are now run as a profit-making enterprise and enable the non-sailor to see and enjoy the harbour from the water.

The problem of access is always with us. There has been only one public jetty where boats can come alongside at all states of the tide. This is at Itchenor and is owned by the Conservancy. Recently a second public jetty has been added at Emsworth. Launch sites are of necessity kept to a minimum as so much of the shoreline of the harbour is mud or privately owned, but there are a small number of hards available for use by those who come down for the day with a boat on a trailer. The locals who feel that the harbour is 'theirs' tend to resent too great an influx of visitors. Parking for cars has been a problem on the Sussex side, but the Conservancy has taken over, extended and improved the car parks at Itchenor and Bosham, the latter through partnership with Chichester District Council. The improvement to the footpaths has enabled many more people to view the harbour from the land and appreciate what is meant by an AONB. In addition, as mentioned earlier, there is the special wheelchair path at Cobnor on the Chidham peninsula. There is always the problem that if a honeypot attracts too many customers, then the peace and beauty which has brought the visitors in the first place is shattered. As Oscar Wilde put it in a different context, 'All men kill the thing they love'.

'... too many people ...'

... most of the threats facing the harbour and its surroundings come from the pressures created by too many people, demanding too much. The demand for development in its various forms and for more opportunities for recreation, and the spiral of increased expectations, combine to create pressures on land and water. Wider roads, larger marinas, more car parks and launching ramps in turn bring more people to the harbour. And in time, unless these pressures are resisted, the harbour will be damaged.

... we believe that one of the most insidious threats to the harbour stems from the attitudes of some of the harbour's users. Most people value the harbour and use it with respect and restraint. But too many either take its beauty for granted, or abuse it ... attitudes can best be changed by awareness and education.

Hence the importance we attach to improving public understanding of the value of the harbour as a national resource, of the threats to the harbour's well-being, and of the need to conserve it.

Managing Chichester Harbour (1993)

When Captain Mackay retired in 1988 his place was taken by Captain John Whitney who had extensive experience of sea service in the Merchant Navy and with Trinity House. He came directly to Chichester Harbour from a previous appointment as Assistant Port Manager and Harbour Master at Weymouth. By the date of his arrival the fairways and mooring trots had been established along the lines first proposed 16 years earlier. The Amenity Area was receiving more attention and was being quoted as an important example of what could be achieved with limited resources. In 1987 the 'Friends of Chichester Harbour' was formed to enable local people with an interest in their locality to put that interest to good use, even though they were

130   Captain John Whitney. Manager and Harbour Master since 1988.

neither members of the Conservancy nor of the Advisory Committee. Today one of the non-statutory places on the latter body is filled by a 'Friend'.

Because agriculture is still one of the more important activities around the harbour, and the farming community is engaged in both the use and protection of the countryside, the Conservancy has recently filled the last non-statutory place on the Advisory Committee with a member of the local farming community.

Since 1990 more has been done. 1992 saw the publication of *The Chichester Harbour Landscape*, with the assistance of the Countryside Commission. In 1993 came the document *Managing Chichester Harbour* and in 1994 the *Chichester Harbour Management Plan*. In this are enshrined the policies of the Conservancy and, in particular, the management principles which the Conservancy has adopted. (See Appendix 3.) Recently the Amenity Officer has been upgraded to the post of Environmental Manager, a part-time Education Officer has been appointed to liaise with school parties and spread the message to children on how to care for their AONB, and new planning guidelines to inform the Conservancy's participation in the town and country planning process have been agreed. Increasingly other areas of the country have looked to Chichester Harbour for ideas on how sensitive areas can be managed in a balanced way.

In 25 years there have been many changes and much progress. Perhaps the secret of the success of the undertaking has been the fact that there have been two bodies associated with

*131   The Conservancy and education. The harbour shoreline is a vast open-air classroom. Here children from West Wittering study the
and dunes and the beach at East Head in 1993. A part-time Education Officer promotes the work of the Conservancy and its rôle in
conservation through work with schools.*

the harbour: the Conservancy which has the executive power and determines how policies
should be carried out and how the money should be spent, and the Advisory Committee composed of harbour users who make suggestions and advise on what might be desirable in the
future. In the case of the yachtsmen, they actually agree to the levels of their own 'taxation'
used to run the harbour—democracy at its finest.

To someone who has seen and been involved in the whole operation it seems amazing
that so much progress has been made in so short a time. Let us hope that the next 25 years will
be as successful as the first.

Sources

Part One—Documents: a select list
Hampshire Record Office, Winchester
Court books, manor of Havant.
Estate papers, Southleigh Park.
Probate records, Havant, Hayling and Warblington.
Portsmouth Central Library
Census returns, Havant, Hayling and Warblington.
Portsmouth City Records Office
Parish records, Havant, Hayling and Warblington.
Shipping records, Portsmouth.
Public Record Office, Kew
Building accounts, Warblington Castle.
Hearth Tax, Hampshire.
Port Books, Port of London.
West Sussex Record Office, Chichester
Census returns, parish and probate records, Apuldram, Birdham, Bosham, Chichester, Chidham, Fishbourne, Itchenor, Thorney, Westbourne, West Wittering.
Chichester Harbour Conservancy records.
Court books, manor of Bosham.
Goodwood Archives, accounts for the sloop *Goodwood*.
Hearth Tax, Rape of Chichester (copies).

Part Two—Books: a select list
J.R. Armstrong, *A History of Sussex* (4th edn. 1995).
G. Bisson (ed.), *The Hampshire Basin and adjoining areas* (4th edn. 1982).
Rita Blakeney, *Fishbourne: A Village History* (1984).
Angela Bromley-Martin, *Bygone Bosham* (1978).
Angela Bromley-Martin, *Chichester Harbour Past & Present* (1991).
Martin Brunnarius, *The Windmills of Sussex* (1979).
Walter Butler, *Topgraphical Account of the Hundred of Bosmere, in Hampshire, comprising the Parishes of Havant, Warblington and Hayling* (1817).
Allen Chandler, *Chichester Harbour: Reflections on Mud and Chi* (2nd edn. 1973).
Gordon T. Copley, *An Archaeology of South-East England* (1958).
Barry Cunliffe, *Fishbourne: A Roman Palace and its Garden* (1971).
James Dallaway, *A History of the Western Division of the County of Sussex*, vol. 1, Rape of Chichester (1815).
Jill Dickin, *Chichester Harbour: The Thirteen Villages* (n.d.).
Martin Doughty (ed.), *Hampshire and D-Day* (1994).

Alec Down, *Roman Chichester* (1988).

Peter Drewett, David Rudling & Mark Gardiner, *The South East to AD 1000* (1988).

John H. Farrant, *The Harbours of Sussex 1700-1914* (1976).

Ian Greig, Kim Leslie & Alan Readman, *D-Day West Sussex: Springboard for the Normandy Landings 1944* (1994).

G. Hamson (ed.), *The Portsmouth Customs Letter Books 1748-1750* (1994).

R.G. Harman, *The Hayling Island Railway* (n.d.).

Thomas Walker Horsfield, *The History, Antiquities and Topography of the County of West Sussex*, vol. 2 (1835).

David Hunn, *Goodwood* (1975).

Richard Joicey, *Langstone: A Mill in a Million* (1976).

Leslie Keating, *The Book of Chichester: A Portrait of the City* (1979).

Anthony Kemp, *Springboard for Overlord: Hampshire and the D-Day Landings* (1984).

Charles John Longcroft, *A Topographical Account of the Hundred of Bosmere in the County of Southampton, including the Parishes of Havant, Warblington and Hayling* (1856).

Rev. J.H. Mee, *Bourne in the Past: Being a History of the Parish of Westbourne* (1913).

D.H. Middleton, *Airspeed: the company and its aeroplanes* (1982).

Roy R. Morgan, *Chichester: A Documentary History* (1992).

G. Morley, *Smuggling in Hampshire and Dorset 1700-1850* (1983).

John Morley, *Old Langstone* (1983).

John Morley, *The Wadeway to Hayling—its history and origins* (1988).

Jeff Morris, *The Story of the Hayling Island Lifeboats* (1989).

Ken Newbury, *The River Lavant* (1987).

Peter Paye, *The Hayling Railway* (1979).

Richard Ratcliff, *A History of Apuldram* (1986).

A.J.C. Reger, *A Short History of Emsworth and Warblington* (1967).

A.J.C. Reger, *Havant & Bedhampton Past & Present* (1975).

David J. Rudkin, *The Hermitage and the Slipper* (1974).

David J. Rudkin, *The Emsworth Oyster Fleet, Industry and Shipping* (1975).

David J. Rudkin, *Old Emsworth* (1978).

David J. Rudkin, *The River Ems and Related Watercourses* (1984).

S.A. Searle, *The Tidal Threat: East Head Spit, Chichester Harbour* (1975).

Keith & Janet Smith, *Witterings Then & Now: West Wittering* (1985).

Keith & Janet Smith, *Birdham & Itchenor Then & Now* (1987).

Barry Stapleton & James H. Thomas, *The Portsmouth Region* (1989).

F.G.S. Thomas, *The King Holds Hayling: An Account of Hayling Island from the Earliest Times* (1961).

Barbara Carpenter Turner, *A History of Hampshire* (2nd edn. 1988).

Victoria County History series:

Hampshire and the Isle of Wight, vols. 1 (1900), 2 (1903), 3 (1908).

Sussex, vols. 1 (1905), 2 (1907), 4 (1953).

P.A.L. Vine, *London's Lost Route to the Sea* (4th edn. 1986).

Mary Waugh, *Smuggling in Kent and Sussex 1700-1840* (1985).

Part Three—Illustrations, Documents and Maps (as numbered in the text)
Alastair Black/PPL, 110
Angela Bromley-Martin, 48-9, 76, 83
Chichester District Museum, 12, 17-18, 54

Appendix 1

Chichester Harbour Conservancy Powers and Duties

The principal piece of legislation defining the powers and duties of the Conservancy is the Chichester Harbour Conservancy Act 1971.

This establishes the Conservancy as the body responsible for the conservancy, maintenance and improvement of the harbour and the amenity area and endows the Conservancy with a wide range of powers, either directly by provisions in the Act, or by incorporating sections of other Acts. In addition, there are a number of other Acts and Regulations which empower the Conservancy, or the Harbour Master. This appendix is not intended to be a comprehensive list of all legislation affecting the Conservancy but is a general guide to its powers and duties.

Chichester Harbour Conservancy Act 1971

Establishes the Conservancy, sets out its main powers and duties, in respect of navigation, moorings, works, dredging, wrecks, house boats, pleasure craft, staff acquisition of property, harbour charges, debt recovery.

Ancillary powers include provision of housing, buildings, vehicles, plant, machinery, holding of shows, exhibitions, regattas, provision of hostels, caravan sites, baths, lavatories and wash houses, accommodation for meals and refreshment, car parking, publicity and information centres and levying of charges.

National Parks and Access to the Countryside Act 1949

Various sections included by the Conservancy's Act relating to nature reserves, access agreements, tree planting, derelict land, byelaws, wardens, appropriation and disposal of land.

Countryside Act 1968

Various sections included by the Conservancy's Act relating to country parks and commons, sailing, boating, bathing and fishing, camping and picnic sites, traffic regulation orders, byelaws and wardens.

Wildlife and Countryside Act 1981

Amends some of the provisions in the above two Acts.

Harbour Docks and Piers Clauses Act 1847

Various sections incorporated into the Conservancy's Act relating to port and harbour functions, vessels, rates and tolls and the collection thereof, distraint and sale of ships and tackle, directions of the Harbour Master, wrecks, obstructions, loading and unloading of vessels, navigation marks and byelaws.

Merchant Shipping Act 1894
Establishes the Conservancy as the local lighthouse authority and imposes responsibilities in respect of navigation marks and their maintenance.

The Acquisition of Land Act (Authorisation Procedure) Act 1946
Enables the Conservancy to compulsorily purchase land.

Local Government Act 1972
Provisions relating to members' and officers' interests.

Public Bodies (Admission to Meetings) Act 1960
Provisions relating to meetings of the Conservancy to be open to press and public.

Harbours Act 1964
Various powers relating to the setting and collection of harbour dues.
Various other maritime legislation relating to Pilotage, Prevention of Collision at Sea, Maritime Security, Marine and Environmental Pollution.

Source: *Chichester Harbour Management Plan*, Appendix 2 (1994)

Appendix 2

Chichester Harbour Conservancy Membership

The Conservancy

West Sussex County Council	4 Members
Hampshire County Council	4 Members
Havant Borough Council	2 Members
Chichester District Council	2 Members
Advisory Committee	3 Members

The Advisory Committee

Royal Yachting Association	1 Member
Chichester Harbour Federation	4 Members
Sussex Sea Fisheries Committee	1 Member
Emsworth Fishermen's Federation	1 Member
English Nature	1 Member
Countryside Commission	1 Member
The Sports Council	1 Member
Chichester District Association of Local Councils	1 Member
British Marine Industries Federation interests	1 Member
Residents	1 Member
Amateur Fishing	1 Member
Naturalists	1 Member
Wildfowlers	1 Member
Friends of Chichester Harbour	1 Member
Farmers and Landowners	1 Member

Source: *Chichester Harbour Management Plan*, Appendix 3 (1994).

Appendix 3

Chichester Harbour Conservancy Management Principles

(a) To ensure that, through the wise use of Chichester Harbour AONB, the management of the various uses and pressures shall be carried out in such a way that ensures the undiminished continuity and replenishment of the whole.

(b) To aim to ensure the greatest continuous benefit to present generations compatible with the needs of future generations and the natural properties of the area. The concepts of sustainability and stewardship over the AONB as a whole form the basis of this plan.

(c) To maintain the harbour for sailing and recreation. To conserve its beauty and to maintain and improve the natural habitat. To manage people pressure. To maintain the harbour as a place for quiet enjoyment and to resist damaging development.

(d) To maintain a balance between the various interests of the harbour users.

(e) To encourage restraint in the way that the harbour is used.

(f) To retain the quiet, undeveloped nature of parts of the Amenity Area, to guard these against pressure for greater access and to avoid the over-management of such areas.

(g) To increase public awareness, particularly among young people, of the value of the harbour and the threats to its well-being.

(h) To undertake a programme of scientific research as the basis for sound environmental management.

(i) To purchase or lease land within the AONB to improve nature conservation and landscape value and to provide for the Conservancy's operational requirements.

(j) To ensure that the Conservancy has an effective role in the structure and local planning process and to maintain a close liaison with the local planning authorities.

(k) To develop a close working partnership with other bodies involved in the harbour and AONB: the County, Borough and District Councils, NRA and Southern Water Services, and the various yachting, land owning, commercial, naturalist and environmental organisations; and to coordinate policy with the other agencies involved in coastal zone management.

(l) To seek high standards of public safety.

(m) To carry out Conservancy policies openly through consultation.

(n) To serve all the harbour and AONB users effectively.

Source: *Chichester Harbour Management Plan*, Chapter 3 (1994).

Appendix 4

Chichester Harbour Conservancy Chairmen, Officers and Freemen

Chairmen of the Conservancy

Vice-Admiral Sir Geoffrey Thistleton-Smith, KBE,CB,GM,DL	1971-75
David Pumfrett	1975-78
Martin Beale, OBE, JP	1978-81
John Reger	1981-84
Mrs Elizabeth Clarke	1984-87
Nigel Pusinelli, CMG, OBE, MC	1987-90
Lieutenant-Commander Richard Wilson, RN	1990-93
Lieutenant-Colonel David Jones	1993-

Chairmen of the Advisory Committee

Colonel Boris Garside, MC	1971
Martin Beale, OBE, JP	1972-78
Geoffrey Calvert	1978-92
Sir Jeremy Thomas, KCMG	1992-

Clerks

Geoffrey Godber, CBE, DL	1971-75
Michael Holdsworth	1975-

Deputy Clerks

David Durbin	1971-83
John Godfrey	1983-

Treasurers

Cecil Mallinson	1971-73
Brian Fieldhouse	1973-89
Paul Rigg	1989-95
Mrs Helen Kilpatrick	1995-

Harbour Masters

Lieutenant-Commander Frederick Hard, RN	1971-74
Captain Ian Mackay, RN (Manager/Harbour Master)	1974-88
Captain John Whitney (Manager and Harbour Master)	1988-

Freemen

Freemanship of the harbour is awarded to individuals who have made an outstanding personal contribution to the management and well-being of the harbour. Freemen are entitled to fly the Conservancy's house flag and to display a special harbour dues paid plaque.

Captain Ian Mackay, RN	April 1988
Martin Beale, OBE, JP	July 1988
Mrs Elizabeth Clarke	July 1988
Mrs Joan Edom	July 1988
Geoffrey Godber, CBE, DL	July 1988
John Reger	July 1988
Mrs Geraldine Mason	July 1989
Nigel Pusinelli, CMG, OBE, MC	July 1990
Geoffrey Calvert	November 1992
David Durbin	November 1992
Robert Hanson	November 1992
Ian Odin	November 1992
Squadron-Leader Anthony Ross, LVO	November 1992
Lieutenant-Commander Richard Wilson, RN	July 1993
Gerald Hurst	May 1994
Captain David Bromley-Martin, RN	January 1995

Appendix 5

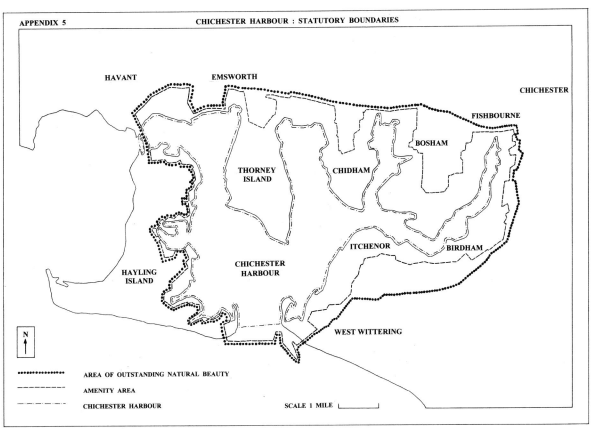

APPENDIX 5   CHICHESTER HARBOUR : STATUTORY BOUNDARIES

HAVANT   EMSWORTH

CHICHESTER

FISHBOURNE

BOSHAM

THORNEY ISLAND

CHIDHAM

ITCHENOR   BIRDHAM

HAYLING ISLAND

CHICHESTER HARBOUR

WEST WITTERING

N

•••••••• AREA OF OUTSTANDING NATURAL BEAUTY

– – – – – AMENITY AREA

–·–·–·– CHICHESTER HARBOUR

SCALE 1 MILE

132

Index